Finding China's Lost Generation

ASIAN VOICES

An Asia/Pacific/Perspectives Series

Series Editor: Mark Selden

Finding China's Lost Generation

The Beijing Fifty-five

John Israel

ROWMAN & LITTLEFIELD
Lanham • Boulder • New York • London

Published by Rowman & Littlefield
An imprint of The Rowman & Littlefield Publishing Group, Inc.
4501 Forbes Boulevard, Suite 200, Lanham, Maryland 20706
www.rowman.com

86-90 Paul Street, London EC2A 4NE, United Kingdom

British Library Cataloguing in Publication Information Available

Library of Congress Cataloging-in-Publication Data

Names: Israel, John, 1935- author.
Title: Finding China's lost generation: the Beijing fifty-five / John Israel.
Description: Lanham, Maryland: Rowman & Littlefield, [2023] | Series: Asian voices | Includes index.
Identifiers: LCCN 2022053811 (print) | LCCN 2022053812 (ebook) | ISBN 9781538174241 (cloth) | ISBN 9781538174258 (paperback) | ISBN 9781538174265 (epub)
Subjects: LCSH: Zhiqing generation—China—Beijing—History. | China—History—Cultural Revolution, 1966–1976.
Classification: LCC HQ799.C552 B464 2023 (print) | LCC HQ799.C552 (ebook) | DDC 305.2350951/156—dc23/eng/20221212
LC record available at https://lccn.loc.gov/2022053811
LC ebook record available at https://lccn.loc.gov/2022053812

Contents

Preface

In 1968, a middle school girl in Xishuangbanna—commonly known as Banna—on China's southwest border obeyed Mao Zedong's edict to "receive re-education from the poor and lower middle peasants" by laboring in a nearby village. There, Li Xiaoliang met several older teenagers who had journeyed from far-off Beijing to work on a local state farm. Her new friends told her how they had voluntarily abandoned educational and professional opportunities in China's capital for a life of backbreaking labor of leveling tropical forests and carving rubber plantations out of a wilderness.

Excited to discover contemporaries with a common identity working in this remote borderland, Beijing-born Xiaoliang invited some of her new friends to her home in the nearby prefectural capital for a warm-hearted reception from her mother—who provided conversation, compassion, and soul food. Guests, in exchange, regaled the Li family with tales of escape from the turmoil of the Cultural Revolution to the challenges of a new frontier.

Nearly thirty years later, Xiaoliang mentioned this group of intrepid Beijing pioneers—who had gained fame in China as the "Fifty-five Educated Youth"—to her husband, a University of Virginia history professor who was researching twentieth-century Chinese education and student movements. Her bewildered spouse (the present author—in case you haven't guessed) confessed that he had never heard of them but vowed to fill the lamentable gap in his professional knowledge. This volume is the product of his efforts.

Having lit a candle, Xiaoliang built a bridge, linking me up to a Fifty-fiver who had settled in Philadelphia. Thanks to this woman's introductions, I have been able to meet several dozen survivors of the group, primarily in Beijing but also elsewhere in China and in the United States, many of whom agreed to interviews and provided access to diaries, blogs, and photos. Now, having shared in the lives of these remarkable individuals for a quarter of a century, I am ready to tell their stories.

Here is the latest in a series of studies I have conducted on students and education in China during the eras of Chiang Kai-shek and Mao Zedong.

Throughout my career I have become increasingly addicted to oral history, which enables the writer to mobilize interviews in the pursuit of scholarship. In this case, I have gone a step further, allowing my sources to speak in their own voices.

Without the face-to-face intercultural interactions made possible by developments following the 1979 normalization of Sino-US relations, such an undertaking would have been unthinkable. During four decades of intermittent residing, teaching, and studying in China, in addition to part-time work as a China-based columnist for the Voice of America's Mandarin-language service, I have enjoyed countless opportunities to learn about Chinese life from the people who live it.

The Chinese refer to urban intellectuals sent to the countryside during the 1960s and 1970s as "Zhishi Qingnian" ("Educated Youth"), "*zhiqing*" for short. This cohort, an estimated seventeen million in number, has already provided material for more than a few scholarly volumes, most notably Michel Bonnin's magisterial *The Lost Generation*. The "Fifty-five"—though by no means typical—enable us to identify a few faces in the crowd. The fact that most of these men and women are still alive, accessible, and articulate enhances their allure. Having established links in the 1990s, returning to Beijing in 2018 for an additional round of interviews, I further discovered that some of them had played vital roles in China's dramatic transformation from an impoverished socialist economy to a world powerhouse. Their stories offer penetrating insights into how the China of Mao Zedong morphed into the China of Xi Jinping.

In addition to interviews, the Fifty-fivers have documented their experience in diaries, memoirs, and blogs. I draw freely from these, seeking, wherever possible to tell their stories in their own words. Extensive quotations are presented as block quotations.

When several interviewees insisted that I eschew the use of their real names, I decided to employ *noms de plume* for everyone in the group—with four exceptions: Ling Yu and Wang Kaiping perished during their Yunnan years. These deaths—Ling's due to illness; Wang's in an accident—were tragic results of the young volunteers' selfless dedication. The third—Yin Zheng, a model worker in his youth who died shortly after our interview—is often lumped with the other two as a heroic exemplar. Since none are still alive but all have become revered historical figures, it would be pointless to present them as anyone but themselves. The fourth, Peng Zhenge, has published a detailed firsthand account of his experience on the State Farm. Because his book, *Dage Bushi Cui Niupi* (*No Bull from Big Brother*), does not attempt to conceal the author's identity, I have followed suit. Block quotations in my account, unless otherwise identified, are taken from this work.

Chapter 1

Children of the Revolution

Born between 1946 and 1951, they were members of the first generation to grow up in postrevolutionary China. Their parents, destinies forged in the cauldron of Japanese invasion and civil war, were working in the capital of the newly founded People's Republic of China (PRC).

Fathers and mothers had made their way to Beijing via two routes. Many had demonstrated loyalty by enlisting in the Communist cause during the anti-Japanese war and civil war that set the stage for the new order. Others had proven themselves useful by contributing knowledge acquired in the classroom and on the job. Defined by whether their professional trajectories were determined mainly by political loyalties or by specialized skills, parents were, in the lingo of the day, either "Red" or "Expert." More than a few were both.

Typical "Red" parents had joined the Communists in Yan'an, the wartime base where Mao Zedong mobilized young men and women eager to join a patriotic struggle against Japan. Chen Gang's father, a high school graduate from Anhui province, arrived in 1938. In Yan'an he met Chen's mother, who had studied in Beijing, moved to Chongqing (Chiang Kai-shek's wartime capital), and come to the Communist base with a student propaganda brigade. Both ended up in the People's Publishing House—where their son eventually pursued a career.

He Longkang's Shanxi-born father, an anti-Japanese student activist and stalwart of the Northwest Youth National Salvation Association, had found his calling in the Yan'an publishing world. After V-J Day, he was sent to the Northeast to help expand the revolution into areas wrested from the Japanese. There he met and married He's mother, a fellow Party worker. He Longkang was born in 1947. After "Liberation"—the official term for the establishment of the new order—his father worked his way up to the number two position in the People's Literature Publishing House.

Liu Xing's father had been a student at the Baoding Normal School—a renowned "cradle of revolution"—where he had joined the Party underground

1

and thrown himself into the National Salvation Movement. Following training in Yan'an, he had been sent to the Taihangshan guerrilla base, where he
joined forces with Liu's mother, a younger activist. Rising through the ranks,
he eventually was chosen as director of the General Office of the Ministry
of Mining.

Li Saiyang was born into a Hunan peasant household that had been initiated into the revolution together with Mao Zedong's teacher, Xu Teli, under
whose tutelage he had found his way to Yan'an. There he married a landlord's
daughter who was also undergoing revolutionary education in the Communist
capital. In 1947, as Yan'an was abandoned to advancing Guomindang forces,
Saiyang and his sister were withdrawn on mule-back, mouths muffled to
prevent them from crying and exposing their position to the enemy. After the
establishment of the new order, Li's father was appointed secretary to head
of the Supreme Procuratorate.

Few Fifty-fivers could boast of more sterling revolutionary credentials than
Zeng Silai. Zeng's tenant farmer father had joined the cause at age thirteen
and worked his way through the ranks to become a People's Liberation Army
(PLA) general.

Wang Qianyun's parents were early converts to the revolution, joining in
the late 1920s. Both had been imprisoned by the Guomindang while recruiting Party members in Chiang Kai-shek's "White Areas." After Liberation his
father served as vice-governor of Shandong.

Homes of several Fifty-fivers had been reconstituted from the detritus of
revolution and civil war. On the eve of Liberation, Wang Sulin's father, a
conscript in Chiang Kai-shek's army, was herded on board a troop transport
and shipped off to Taiwan. After a decade of waiting in vain for word from
her exiled spouse, his mother was remarried to an older official. Lin Ping's
father, similarly, was dragooned aboard a Taiwan-bound vessel shortly after
her birth. After hearing nothing from him for ten years, her mother had also
married an older cadre.

Some families bore the scars of recent violence. Li Xiansu's mother
had survived the death of two husbands—the first killed by the Japanese,
the second (one of her martyred spouse's comrades-in-arms) executed by
Chiang Kai-shek's subordinate Fu Zuoyi before he surrendered Beijing to the
Liberation Army. Her mother eventually married a cadre who had, similarly,
lost his spouse during the civil war. Xiansu's new father brought into the family an older stepbrother and stepsister. Since her mother was preoccupied with
parenting stepchildren, Xiansu was raised by a nursemaid.

The Peng brothers, Zhenge and Aidi, had roots outside China's borders.
Their father came from a Hakka family that had lived in Southeast Asia since
the nineteenth century. Returning to China after the Japanese invasion to help
build the Burma Road, he was introduced to Zhou Enlai, who paved his way

to Yan'an. There he met the Pengs' mother, an ethnic Mongolian similarly attracted to the patriotic cause. Peng père had served as a post-Liberation overseas Chinese representative on the People's Political Consultative Council, where he helped in the selection of the revolutionary regime's flag and national anthem.

Intellectuals constituted the most substantial subgroup among the Fifty-fivers' families. Though most of these well-educated parents also served the government in one way or another, they honed their social position and political image via learning and specialized knowledge rather than political and military exploits.

Some held both intellectual and political credentials. An Zhenke's father, a professor at the Beijing College of Commerce, had gone to France to participate in the work-study program spearheaded by Zhou Enlai and Deng Xiaoping. Upon his return, he had transformed his handicraft cooperative into a front organization for underground Party work.

Mao Zedong's New China was compelled to draw upon skills stockpiled in the pre-PRC era. Sun Ling's father had studied chemical engineering at Central University in Chongqing where Chiang Kai-shek himself served as chancellor. Adding to Mr. Sun's compromised credentials was the fact that his older brother had settled in Taiwan. Sun's father was, nonetheless, appointed senior engineer in the Ministry of Chemical Engineering.

Another engineer who made the transition from the old order to the new was Zhou Chanshen's father. Having helped to plan the pre-Liberation Guiyang-Kunming railroad, he went on to play key roles, post-1949, in erecting the famous bridges spanning the Yangzi at Wuhan and Nanjing.

Huang Qianzu's maternal grandfather had studied with Zhang Jian, a renowned early twentieth-century industrialist reformer who had pioneered the modern textile industry in the lower Yangzi valley. His father, a rural intellectual, after graduating from the renowned Nantong Textiles College, had gone on to carve a career as a professor and engineer in the Ministry of Textiles. Seeing the Communist Party as an instrument of seismic change, he joined the Chinese Communist Party (CCP) shortly after Liberation.

Su Baikai's epileptic father was confined to his brother's home, where young Su was raised. Su's uncle, though a Guomindang functionary, was supportive of China's revolutionary rulers. Su recalls having been raised in a "feudal" culture. Younger children were forbidden to sit at the dinner table. During Chinese New Year and other holidays, the kids could not start eating until adults had lifted their chopsticks. When helping oneself to food from the common bowl, a child was not permitted to pick and choose choice morsels. "The pattern of obedience," recalled Su, "was drilled into my head":

> Obedience to the teacher, obedience to the Party. I really didn't have much capacity for independent judgment. I was the boy who couldn't say "no." Here we see the influence both of Chinese tradition and of my particular family.

Though Su's may have been an extreme case, the patriarchal authoritarianism, hierarchy, and discipline that he recalls permeated the homes of many Fifty-fivers. Though Party and State hoped to mold a new generation of revolutionary youth, child-raising responsibilities remained anchored in the family. Parental discipline and political control were mutually reinforcing.

Most Fifty-fivers grew up enjoying a comfortable standard of urban life, but none reached the level of luxury recalled by Lu Heman. The Lu family's prominence dated from the Qing dynasty (1644–1911). Lu's was the eighth generation to receive an advanced education. His paternal grandfather had been a prominent mathematician. His grandfather, though poor and self-educated, had served as director of Education for Hebei province during the late Qing and eventually became a philanthropist-reformer whose contributions helped to build Nankai—China's most famous non-sectarian private university.

Lu recalls a childhood in a Tianjin mansion with wooden floors and French windows where milk, bread, and butter were daily fare, imported cheese a routine snack. Even after relocating to Beijing, until the 1960s the Lu family employed two nannies. Having trained in the United States to fly P-47s in the anti-Japanese struggle, after the war's end Lu's father had gone over to the Communists. As a civil aviation pilot, he brought home a salary of five hundred renminbi a month—a princely sum in post-Liberation China. "For my tenth birthday," recalls Lu,

> my mother had some of my friends over for a party featuring Kiessling's ice cream, the most famous brand in Tianjin. The Kiessling employee delivered a tub of it. We all sat around a large table eating ice cream and when we had finished, the employee gave each of us another scoop. The ten yuan spent on the tub of Kiessling's could have supported the average Tianjin resident for a month.

A handful of Fifty-fivers had similarly grown up in homes with cosmopolitan trappings. Li Man's house was decorated with objets d'art that her diplomat father had carried back from postings in Yemen, Zambia, and other countries. The father of Wu Ning and Wu Sibing, the only sister/brother pair among the Fifty-five, was an aviator who had returned to the Mainland from Hong Kong in 1949 and built a career in aviation administration. Zhang Cunlong's father had also been in Hong Kong at the time of the revolution, working in international maritime trade. Having delayed return to his motherland until

1951, he had remained under a shadow because of his close connection to the international world of capitalist commerce.

Although China's new rulers deemed themselves surrogates of the working class, few of the Fifty-five could claim proletarian roots. A notable exception was Li Zhenzhan, whose construction worker dad had married a village teacher encountered in the northwest frontier province of Xinjiang. After his father's death, his mother had taken young Li back to her native Beijing where she had grown up in a Manchu family.

In sum, the Fifty-fivers' families constituted a cross-section of Beijing's white-collar urbanites whose loyalty, skills, and hard work underpinned the new order in China's capital.

Chapter 2

School Days

Fifty-fivers attended primary school during the PRC's early years. Besides drilling in the pedagogical basics, pupils were expected to absorb—as much as they could at an early age—Chinese Marxism's ideological nostrums, including an understanding of history that stressed class struggle, the redemptive role of the Communist Party, and both the desirability and inevitability of world revolution under the leadership of the Soviet Union. School authorities also channeled students' energies toward physical fitness and sports.

Interviewed in the 1990s, members of China's first postrevolutionary generation viewed their childhoods in stark contrast to the current period of post-Maoist reform. Looking back from the era of "opening up and reform" in which children feel compelled—as early as kindergarten or even nursery school—to focus on a series of ruthless elimination contests culminating in the university entrance exams, academic life prior to the Cultural Revolution seemed idyllic. To be sure, primary school matriculants had to survive competitive exams to gain entry to elite middle—followed by high—schools and, hopefully, universities. For families privileged to harvest the fruits of revolution, however, there was little doubt that the socialist state would provide a secure future.

In the mid-1950s, youthful optimism, harmony, and sense of security were vitiated by a series of crises. In the summer of 1957, the regime marked for punishment those who had spoken out during the brief period of liberalization called the Hundred Flowers Movement. Individuals who had answered Mao's call to criticize Party policies were denounced as "Rightists" and shipped to remote locations for "reform through labor." Wang Xiaoyun's father had been a Party member for three decades, remaining steadfast even while imprisoned by the Guomindang. Straightforward and without guile, he had taken at face value the invitation to voice grievances under the Hundred Flowers umbrella. His reward: demotion from vice-governor of Shandong province to factory manager in a small industrial town. Not until 1964 was he exonerated and allowed to return to Beijing.

The father of the Peng brothers, Zhenge and Aidi, held a high-level post in the Overseas Chinese Affairs office. However, a Western colonial upbringing and connections to overseas Chinese left him vulnerable to charges that he was less than a hundred percent loyal. In 1958 both parents were labeled "Rightists" and exiled to a farm on remote Hainan Island. Zhenge's first inkling that something was wrong came when his mother informed him that he was henceforth to be head of the family. The eleven-year-old boy had already been transferred out of the Yucai Primary School, an elite institution for children of high officials. Now he and his little brother were driven from their commodious quarters and crammed into a dingy room, where they remained until their parents' return more than a year later. Even after his father's and mother's exoneration, Zhenge remained ineligible for Young Communist League membership because he had failed to "draw a line" between himself and his "reactionary" family.

Though most children did not suffer the ignominy of parents vilified, persecuted, and exiled, the Anti-Rightist Movement cast a pall over the world of political and intellectual elites in which most of the Fifty-five were living. Children, already wary of any sign of "bourgeois" thought or behavior in their homes, now had cause for profound crises of identity.

Having purged suspected dissidents, Mao and his confederates turned for help to individuals conspicuous for ideological zeal rather than specialized knowledge, in keeping with the Great Leap Forward, a nationwide movement to modernize from the bottom up. Now the urban elite found their comfortable foundations shaken. Middle and high schools where the Fifty-five were studying witnessed an influx of less cultivated classmates admitted because of "revolutionary" family status and ideological purity rather than academic achievement. But the Great Leap Forward's most devastating impact on China's urban population was a critical food shortage, beginning in 1959 and extending into the early 1960s, the result of plummeting supplies of grain, oil, meat, and other commodities brought on by natural disasters compounded by administrative chaos. Though spared the famine that claimed tens of millions of rural lives, China's urban population, including residents of the nation's capital, survived on short rations. It was not a happy time.

Following recovery from the famine, Mao Zedong moved to prevent power and policy from slipping into the hands of a bureaucratic elite operating on a Soviet "revisionist" model. Assisted by hand-picked Minister of Defense Lin Biao, the chairman presided over a series of movements to purify ideology and guarantee the nation's adherence to a socialist model of development. Students were mobilized to adulate heroic martyrs, focus loyalty on the supreme leader, and reaffirm commitment to Maoist doctrines.

MIDDLE SCHOOL AND HIGH SCHOOL

Before setting out for Yunnan in February 1968, the "Fifty-five" (in fact totaling fifty-eight) had been enrolled in some twenty-two institutions, most of them in Beijing's eastern district—thirteen, ages thirteen to sixteen in middle schools; forty-five, ages seventeen to nineteen in high schools.

Nine of the boys had just finished the third and final year at Beijing's No. 25 High School. This renowned academy traced its history to 1864 when its antecedent—Yuying High—was founded by American Congregationalist missionaries. During the 1950s No. 25 had established ties with the Wilhelm Pieck School, named after the president of the German Democratic Republic ("East Germany"). Pieke had officially donated one of its buildings.

Figure 2.1. Beijing's No. 25 High School. (image.baidu.com)

A still larger number, eleven boys and four girls, were studying at an off-shoot of No. 25—No. 65—established in 1955. Located behind the Museum of Fine Arts and a stone's throw from Beijing's shopping hub, No. 65 was the capital's only high school that did not include a middle school component.

Though China's revolutionary lexicon did not include the term "prep school," No. 65 was designed for the college-bound, drawing applicants from homes of well-placed officials and intellectuals. Many students, including some of the Fifty-five, were graduates of Beijing's most rigorous schools.

Among them could be found sons and daughters of members of the CCP's Central Committee, the Cabinet, the Beijing city administration, bureau and section heads, as well as kids who lived in the compounds of the Ministry of Foreign Affairs, the CCP's Propaganda Bureau, security organs, and military bases. Only a few came from families of higher intellectuals. In this institution that prided itself on its scholarly standards, most successful applicants were, whatever their family background, academic achievers.

The No. 5 High School, also ranked among the most selective of Beijing's secondary educational institutions, was home to six of the Fifty-five.

Although no other institution enrolled more than a couple of Fifty-fivers, worthy of mention is No. 101 High School, which embodied many ideals of the new revolutionary order. Situated on the grounds of the Old Summer Palace in the Haidian District where Beida, Qinghua, and other famous universities were clustered, No. 101 was an exclusive high school for sons of high officials. Most graduates went on to the top-secret Harbin Military Engineering Academy. The school ethos of No. 101, recalled one graduate, was "collectivism and militarism." Two Fifty-fivers—Liu Xing and Lai Weijin—attended No. 101.

In keeping with the mantra of "The Three Goods" (Academic/Moral/Physical), a severe bodily disability could prevent an otherwise promising student from advancing to higher levels of learning. Furthermore, since "Moral" included politics, students with exemplary family backgrounds enjoyed advantages in gaining admission to schools of their choice.

In middle and high school, as in primary school, students prepared for a series of rigorous examinations to weed out those qualified to continue to higher levels. Getting into one of Beijing's better institutions was largely a matter of academic achievement and test scores. Enrollment in prestigious high schools ensured a smooth transition to a university. For sons and daughters of Beijing's prominent officials, prospects for success appeared ever within reach.

Academic requirements, though demanding, were seldom all-consuming. In addition to intramural and intermural sports, there were breaks for "voluntary labor," even for primary school pupils mobilized to perform simple operations in small factories. Beginning in middle school and continuing through high school, youngsters were routinely sent to help peasants in nearby villages bring in the harvest.

Virtually all activities had political overtones. In the weeks leading up to the October 1 National Day, schools focused on preparation for Mao's Tiananmen Square review. Young enthusiasts understood that good deeds that "served the people" would be taken into account when they applied for coveted membership in the Young Communist League (YCL). Misfortunates from families of questionable political and social class backgrounds found that heroic efforts were required. Every day for nearly two months, Peng Andi burnished their political credentials by shouldering buckets of cesspool human wastes.

POLITICAL SOCIALIZATION

Youth growing up in New China were trained to be loyal citizens, proud of their country, supportive of revolutionary socialist values, ready to serve the national cause, and, if necessary, to risk lives for the motherland.

China's political socialization was more profound, more persistent, and more penetrating than anything familiar to children raised in Western democratic societies. Compared to the experience of youngsters raised in New China, the ritualistic indoctrination of American students—standing, pledging allegiance, and reading patriotic histories—is weak tea.

Political training began in the classroom. Teachers were vetted and textbooks were edited for political correctness. A key figure in the school administration was the Party secretary who enjoyed powers equal to—and often superior to—that of the principal. Teachers and a handful of high school students might be admitted to the Party. After reaching the age of fifteen, everyone vied for admission to the YCL. Virtually all primary and middle school students wore the red scarf of the Young Pioneers. To be excluded from the Pioneers was more than a sign of political disloyalty. It marked the individual as unworthy of equal peer group status.

Indoctrination flowed through many channels. Students were shown films depicting their nation's recent history of glorious revolutionary struggle under ever-correct Party leadership. Schools promoted nationwide campaigns to publicize the exploits of young heroes and heroines who had lived their lives in service of Party, State, and Revolution.

Political lessons learned in school were reinforced at home. Most Fifty-fivers' families had participated in the revolutionary struggle or at least supported the new regime once it took power. Even when speaking to children behind closed doors, parents knew full well that the most oblique criticism of the official line might come back to haunt them. Finally, quite apart from conforming to Party or State dictates, parents taught children—as had Chinese parents through the ages—that the teacher was always right.

THE DIARY OF A YOUNG GIRL

Vivid images of student life emerge through the diary of one of the younger members of the Fifty-five, Li Juxing, known better by her nickname, "Little

Li." Born in December 1950, Little Li was a middle school student in the 1965–1966 school year leading up to the Cultural Revolution. On August 25, 1965, she prefaced her journal with two quotations, the first from a Soviet novelist, the second from an exemplar of Maoist values:

> Man's dearest possession is Life. It is given to him but once, and he must live it so as to feel no torturing regrets for wasted years, never know the burning shame of a mean and petty past. Live so that, dying, one might say: all my life, all my strength were given to the finest cause in all the world—the fight for the Liberation of Mankind.—Nikolai Ostrovsky, author, *How the Steel Was Tempered*

> To eat you need food, to fight you need weapons, to drive you need a steering wheel, to make revolution you need The Works of Chairman Mao.—Lei Feng

> Today is the first day of school. This semester I must study hard, positively reconstruct my thought. . . . Strive to get admitted to the Communist Youth League [CYL] as soon as possible.

Moral:

1. Study the Works of Mao and do everything I can to put them into practice.
2. Positively participate in collective activities.
3. Study relevant documents of CYL etc.
4. Act with determination to correct my shortcoming of not loving to help others.

Intellectual:

1. Study hard and to the point.
2. Don't put off until tomorrow what I should do today.
3. Conduct a weekly review of my classes, turning the classroom into a battlefield, treating lessons as the enemy.

Little Li is a puritan, consumed by guilt at having failed to live up to the high standards she has set for herself. These standards are both political and personal, both instrumental and absolute. If she hopes to realize her academic promise and succeed in life, she must earn good grades. If she seeks to gain admission to the highly selective CYL, she must be a political exemplar. But Little Li is no mere opportunist. She is driven by a sense of personal inadequacy based upon shame for belonging to the wrong social class and by a will to succeed inextricably linked to revolutionary goals defined by the CCP.

Inspired by the portrait of Chairman Mao at the front of the classroom, Little Li relentlessly wrestles with the underlying problem—her low political consciousness. Having accepted Mao's mandate to sacrifice for a greater cause, she concludes:

> It seems that I haven't fully adopted the idea of serving the people and rooted it firmly in my brain. Individualism keeps raising its ugly head. From now on I must do everything I can to elevate myself upward.

Little Li's guilty conscience has focused upon a new issue: She has been asked to participate in an intermediate-distance race that takes more talent and effort than she can offer. She resents being picked out for a demanding but menial task. Who is responsible for such self-indulgent feelings? None other than herself!

> It's my capitalist thought. . . . I've forgotten Chairman Mao's words: "Serve the people." Since focusing on the sprint would be of little use to the people and working on the intermediate distance race, though more demanding, would be of greater use to the people, why shouldn't I be willing to do it? The virtues of the intermediate run are not only in physical training but even more in ideological training. Rather than shrinking back in face of the challenge, why shouldn't I welcome it?
>
> Chairman Mao says, "Work is hard. Wherever it's hardest, that's the place to go."

August 27, 1965

Marching orders have already been issued for the October 1 National Day parade. Third-year students have been delegated to shoulder responsibility for logistics. Little Li is morally obliged to emulate their spirit of dedication.

> With all my heart I must learn from them. With all my heart I must fulfill the responsibility that the Party has given us. Let the people of the world see our younger generation, let the American imperialists see our younger generation. Look at us and make the people of the whole world smile—and make the American imperialists tremble.

August 28, 1965

Sharing a desk with Little Li is a newly arrived student from her hometown of Hangzhou who has fallen behind in her studies.

> She is my comrade, my social class sister. I must stand by her side, work with her, help her catch up. . . . She is young, she is intelligent, more important, she ardently loves the Party, ardently loves Chairman Mao, ardently loves the Red Armband [of the Young Pioneers]. I must learn from her and move forward with her.

August 20, 1965

Back then when our five-starred flag flew above Tiananmen Square for the first time, was blood not still being shed on the front lines? How many loyal sons and daughters sacrificed their Lives over several decades so that we could enjoy our current victory!"—*Anthology from the Distant Realm*

Little Li views herself not simply as a dependent child and diligent student but as a daughter of the New China:

I had just been born. December 1950. The Red Flag was already fluttering in the breeze. Everyone was joyously greeting the new year. I grew up under the flag of the Communist Youth League. How innocent I was of the past! For all I knew they had always had it this good. I went off to school, and thanks to the lessons of my teachers, for the first time I realized that there had been an old society with landlords and capitalists.

Educated by the CYL, I entered my thirteenth year. Only then did I truly come to understand, one step at a time, the realities of the past. I deeply came to appreciate the fact that just as I was coming into this world, the People's Volunteers were protecting us with their flesh and blood. So here I was, this little child, and from the day I was born, I received my fresh life-giving blood from the older generation of revolutionaries. Every step I took was in the blood of our martyrs. But I had initially known nothing of this. All my thoughts were focused on my individual self. Now I know. I must carry on the glorious tradition of my revolutionary forefathers and struggle to the end for the Liberation of the people of the world!

Little Li's universe extends far beyond the walls of the schoolyard. Her sense of purpose is molded by a sense that she is walking in the footsteps of giants:

August 30, 1965

We are whipping ourselves into shape for the Motherland, for the people. Of course it's tough. But what's a little hardship compared with what the Red Army went through [during the Long March of 1934–1935] crossing the Grasslands, surviving on roots of the grass and boiled leather belts? What does a little bit of hardship amount to compared to the People's Volunteers eating noodles covered with snow? Compared with those who are defending world peace, what does this tiny bit of hardship amount to? So, in the calculus of suffering, it is precisely through arduous struggle that revolution moves forward. No arduous struggle, no revolutionary victory!

Little Li's driving sense of purpose follows her everywhere:

August 31, 1965

Each time I go to the park to exercise, I notice a male comrade practicing long distance running. His style is all wrong and his pace is not fast, but somehow he attracts my attention. Why? First of all, he is out there exercising every day, every single day. More important, this guy is the workman who delivers milk. What's a milkman doing working out like this every day? He's not out there to set any records. Nobody is going to sing his praises. Why's he going to all that trouble? It must be because of his dedication to serving the people. He's doing it for the revolution, for the people, for his work. Otherwise, why would he be sweating it out like this?

And why do I work out? It's crystal clear. When I plumb the depths of my soul, I see it plainly enough: It's all in the hope that I will become a famous athlete. That's why I throw in the towel as soon as I encounter the slightest hardship. So today, when I uncovered the most glaring weakness in my exercise routine, I was beside myself with joy.

September 1, 1965

The wind is kicking up, raindrops are starting to fall. We've been running for three hours, and the sky is getting dark. From a distance come the peals of thunder. Yes, the rain must fall, and yet we've only finished half of our mission. Step on the gas! Each of us knows full well that when the Red Army was crossing the Grasslands, it was much worse than this. For our revolutionary forebears, it was much worse than this. Only through hardship can we toughen the sinews of revolution. We are training not only our bodies but our minds. We are putting to the test our revolutionary commitment.

Even before rising from her bed each morning, Little Li is consumed with revolutionary thoughts:

September 2, 1965

It's still dark outside but the Lights have been turned off and the morning bells are ringing. [Cousin] Hailin and I, snuggled up under our quilt, are pouring out hearts and souls to each other. Still under the magical spell cast by our Sino-Japanese friendship rally, we are chatting about the Long March. When the conversation turns to Wang Ruofei and Ye Ting and how they sacrificed themselves for the revolution, we become incomparably sad and our voices fall. But when we talk about Chairman Mao, neither of us can suppress her excitement. You can't see it, but you can feel it in every word we speak. How happy it is, how beautiful, it is, to live in the era of Mao Zedong!

Our school has a glorious revolutionary history. On one of our school anniversaries President Liu visited and wrote an inscription. The *People's Daily* published an article on our school's exploits. The Party has really cared for us, really cared for us! But look at me today. In every respect, I have failed to Live up to the Party's expectations—in my studies, in my thinking, in my physical condition, in absolutely every respect, I have been too soft.

I confront myself with these demands: To give my all to study the Works of Chairman Mao, to be a "Three Good" student, so that Chairman Mao and the older generation can put their minds to rest. We are spending every moment preparing to struggle for the Communist enterprise!

> The Party is my father and mother,
> The Works of Chairman Mao are my guiding Light,
> I must always follow the Party,
> Always wage revolution! Revolution!

September 4, 1965

For Little Li, going to the movies is more than light entertainment. After seeing Long Live the Victory of the People's War, *she reflects:*

Chairman Mao is the people's helmsman, the people's North Star, the people's guiding Light. The Great War of Resistance was a huge victory for Mao Zedong Thought! A huge victory for People's War.

Now American imperialism is waging a war of aggression in Vietnam, seeking to dominate the entire world. But it will end up falling into the sea of fire—People's War—and burning itself to death!

September 8, 1965

Little Li's school has just staged a joint drill with the No. 8 Boys Middle to prepare for the National Day review in Tiananmen Square. The first-year girls marched badly. How can they face Chairman Mao?

September 10, 1965

Without any official authorization, a schoolmate has taken the initiative. What to make of it? Little Li now realizes that any individual can step forward to play an important role. Here is what has happened: In place of afternoon calisthenics, they had a drill. But the instructor had other commitments and couldn't make it. Could they still go ahead with the drill? Suddenly Little Li noticed something unusual:

Dong Lin was standing in front of the formation shouting slogans. She wasn't shouting them particularly well, but she was taking it seriously and sincerely and everybody was following her.

Each slogan reverberated in my breast. I felt ashamed. Dong Lin was just a squad captain. Shouting slogans for drill wasn't her responsibility. Why was she taking command? I thought back to another scene. She was sitting there with furrowed brows engrossed in reading the Selected Works of Mao.

It always seemed that whenever nobody else took charge, she stepped forward. When nobody was there to bark commands at drill, she did it. Nobody to lead the songs, she did. No matter what, so long as she could do it, she just stepped forward and did it. Did it! Did it! Did it! Then I realized that it mattered not what title individuals might or might not hold, so long as they were committed to serving the people, to serving their fellow students, no matter what the task, whether or not they held an official position, they could serve the people. Previously I had always assumed that only a cadre could really serve the people.

Even though I knew this in principle, I never made the mental connection to real Life. In fact, there were so many things that nobody else did that I wanted to do but felt embarrassed to do. So, I was always doing everything I could to dredge up excuses as to why I should not step forth, and I walled myself off. Today she really served as a model for me. Was she not the very embodiment of Lei Feng? The real hero doesn't go around showing off but puts everything she has into serving the people.

In fact, it doesn't make the slightest difference whether you are a cadre or not. In many situations, it just comes down to whether you step forward and get it done! Whether an individual has a lot to contribute or a Little, so long as she has the spirit, so long as she is a noble minded individual, a pure individual, a moral individual, an individual who can rise above the herd, an individual who can benefit the people. Today I have once again come to appreciate the teachings of the Chairman. From now on, I will act according to the principles of the Chairman.

September 11, 1965

This afternoon at 3:00 the second National Athletic Competition opened with a grand ceremony. Our great leader chairman Mao was there. . . . Alas, I had no ticket and could not attend. . . .

Chairman Mao! Chairman Mao! When will I ever get to see you, to receive your instructions through my own ears? Only when I have heard your words, read your writings, acted in accord with your precepts, set out with all my heart to serve the people, only then will I really be able to see you.

This morning, when Hailin and I got out of bed, she told me she had dreamt of Chairman Mao.

Little Li lives in a world of struggle:

September 13, 1965

The classroom is our battlefield, exam questions our fortress, the teacher our commander, the pens in our hands our weapons! Weapons are to kill the enemy, not to protect him! Fight! Fight! Fight for the people! That is what it means to serve the people.

September 14, 1965

Little Li is ever on guard against her tendency to abjure her own responsibilities and blame problems on others. When she holds an inexperienced teacher responsible for her problems learning algebra, she realizes:

> If I totally deny any personal responsibility, am arrogantly proud and turn around and blame everything on the teacher if I can't solve the problem, it's as if I didn't have any responsibility myself. . . . Both the teacher and I are engaged in the learning process for the sake of revolution. When the teacher encounters problems, not only don't I help him and encourage him but, just the opposite, I undermine him. What kind of attitude is that?

September 16, 1965

Little Li is resentful of a classmate who has been named company commander of the Young Pioneers while she is still just an ordinary member. But she knows this is the wrong attitude and thinks of the model Maoist revolutionary Lei Feng. Lei was just an ordinary soldier. He didn't give a hoot for rank. The only important thing was to serve the revolution. He sought only to be a "rustproof screw" in the machinery of revolution.

> In two weeks it will be our National Day. What will I have to show for it? What will be my gift to Chairman Mao and the Party?

Little Li hears it loud and clear: She must be more disciplined! Make every moment count! Above all she must eschew that "shortcoming of the intellectuals"—"mouthing a bunch of empty words and accomplishing little."
Her highest ambition is to get admitted to the CYL. But she questions her own motives:

September 20, 1965

> Communist Youth League members—What kind of people are they? How can I become one? Some people say they won't be admitted to CYL. Right? But they'll carry out the revolution in any case. I'm not altogether clear about this issue.

Every benefit that Little Li receives brings new responsibilities:

September 22, 1965

> Our new dorm is finished, large enough to accommodate a thousand of us, virtually unique among Beijing's high schools. This shows the concern that Chairman Mao has for us and is evidence that our great Motherland is flying

forward. But we don't want to let this go to our heads. We must continue to maintain a Spartan lifestyle. We must continue to wash our own clothes, make our own beds, learn from our uncles in the PLA.

Little Li's world, however, is by no means confined to home and classroom:

September 28, 1965

Hearing [a radio commentary] gave me some understanding of the Vietnam problem and a clearer image of this American imperialist running dog in a human skin. Formerly I thought that since China is so strong, the American imperialists would not dare invade and even if they did, they would only occupy a scorched earth before being driven out by our PLA. And why would they want to bomb our capital, Beijing? As I saw it, American imperialism would only invade small countries. They wouldn't dare attack a big one. But facts have proven me wrong. American imperialism is a mad dog. The dog doesn't choose between the strong and the weak. He bites everyone he sees. But even if he wants to control the entire world, we Chinese will resist him at every turn. And we'll be the mote in his eye.

The American imperialists have occupied Taiwan, they're invading Vietnam, they're shoring up the reactionary clique in India and the Japanese imperialists. All this is to set the stage for invading us. They want to bring war to our soil. But we are not afraid. If they come, we will fight and quickly wipe them out.

There is no line of demarcation between school and battlefield:

For our generation of young people, war is a great school, a grand arena in which we will be put to the test, toughening us up and making us still stronger. It tells us that if we want to support Vietnam, we first and foremost must promote production, protect our battle station—and that battle station is the classroom. The classroom is a battlefield, no more, no less. We absolutely must defend our battle station. Then if, against all odds, war comes to us, we will have even more formidable resources to throw against the enemy.

While ideological absolutes may suffice in analyzing international events, parochial issues such as joining the Young Communist League are more complicated:

September 29, 1965

I hear that our second-year middle school class has been given a quota of two CYL members. I am all aflutter. Who could they be?

When I see others being admitted to the CYL, I am both happy and jealous and a bit ashamed. In two months I'll be fifteen. What do I know of the Corps? How can I get in?

I feel that I'm groping around blindly. I don't know what to do. What is a CY member after all? This evening I'll have to corner our teacher for a heart-to-heart so that I can come up with a solid plan.

Struggle though she may to get into the CYL, on China's National Day, Little Li's most ardent dream comes true: She and her schoolmates are marching to Tiananmen Square to be reviewed by Chairman Mao:

October 1, 1965

"The East is red/the Sun has risen." Our great leader Mao Zedong has gone up to the Tiananmen rostrum. I am standing in the ranks. Though I can't see him, I seem able to sense it: Chairman Mao is on top of the Tiananmen gate and has walked to the very center. Now they are playing the National Anthem. Our five-starred red flags are flying above. I raise my right hand high.

At this moment I feel so proud. The Chinese people have stood up! Stood up! China is standing tall and strong in the East. No more insults from those Westerners! Wow! My great Motherland and I, a flower of the Motherland! I'm so proud I could burst! And I'm standing there, my shoulders thrust high. I want to shout for all the world to hear: "The Chinese people have stood up!"

Mayor Peng Zhen is speaking. We are starting to march. My heart is beating uncontrollably. Chairman Mao, Chairman Mao, in just a minute I'll be able to see you.

We have passed the Zhonghua Gate. We are entering Tiananmen Square. I am gazing up at the Gate of Heavenly Peace, my eyes searching for Chairman Mao. Yes! Chairman Mao! Chairman Mao is there! Standing right in the middle and applauding. He's waving his hand! Long Live Chairman Mao! Long Live Chairman Mao! I'm wildly waving my bouquet of flowers back and forth. But there's no way I can express the feelings welling up in my heart. Oh that I could fly to the side of Chairman Mao! My voice is cracking, tears welling up in my eyes. "Long Live Chairman Mao!" I cry, half shouting, half weeping. How I felt at that moment can't be put into words. Even if I were a great writer, there would be no way to describe how I felt at that moment.

As she prepares to set out to labor in a nearby village, Little Li reflects upon her last two stints. She feels a sense of accomplishment in her productive activities. But the focus should have been on thought reform.

We took our problems with us as we worked. We did not do enough in terms of learning from the exemplary character of the poor and lower middle peasants. We placed too one-sided an emphasis on labor, whereas the main point in going to the village should have been to discipline our minds, to learn from the fine tradition of the poor and lower middle peasants.

Considering, in retrospect, Little Li's subsequent "reeducation at the hands of the poor and lower middle peasants" in Yunnan, these words carry more than a touch of irony.

October 3, 1965

Last stint of physical labor—I never had a chance to think about or experience what arduous struggle is all about, why we are expected to "engage in arduous struggle"?

As to why we should learn from the poor and lower middle peasants and what we were supposed to learn from them, I only came away with a theoretical once-over-lightly. There was no substance to it.

Why should we unite with the workers and peasants? How should we unite? Is there nothing more to uniting than eating together, living together, and working together? If we are expected to unite, we must have workers and peasants to unite with, right? But, in the course of our work, we encountered very few peasants. What are we supposed to do?

And finally, we came away without a clear understanding of exactly what it meant to "serve the people."

During our last stint of labor, I washed my fellow students' clothes and brought them their food. Well and good. I did what I should. But my motives were not pure. I was trying to bring glory to myself. But look, Hu Yuan didn't wash her fellow students' clothes. So how come everyone said she was learning how to put the slogan "serve the people" into practice? Because whatever her fellow students needed, she just did, without consideration of fame or fortune. And for me, when I noticed that students praised anyone who brought food, I went out of my way to bring food. When I saw that they praised anyone who washed clothes, I washed clothes. To put it in a nutshell, anything that elicited my fellow students' praise, I did. It was nothing but formalism. My idea of what it meant to serve the people was too limited. Serving the people is not just doing good deeds. Study, physical training, and even eating, are all ways of serving the people.

This is pretty strong stuff. Little Li is trying to live her young life on multiple levels. She wants to obey, to do exactly what is expected of her. On the other hand, she cannot be content with ritualistic conformity. What she sees beneath the surface is profoundly disturbing. The combination of physical activism and psychological introspection have infused self-doubt into to the hectic life and guilty conscience of this Beijing middle school student.

Every day I read Mao's *Selected Works*, focus my study on "Serve the People," "In Memory of Norman Bethune," "An Analysis of China's Social Classes," "Against Liberalism," and "The Foolish Old Man Who Moved Mountains." I try to get to the roots: *Why* should we serve the people? What is my motive? Is there, perhaps, some individual calculation lurking therein? Where am I showing off where I shouldn't—or failing to strut my stuff where I should? And why? What should I do from now on? Advance upward or run around like a chicken with my head cut off? Screw up my courage to struggle or beat a hasty retreat?

November 21, 1965

After attending my politics class, I am even more deeply aware of the heavy burden placed upon my shoulders. So many people's eyes are focused on us. So many people are placing their hopes upon us. They are saying, "So long as there is a China, there is still hope for the world's revolution."

Little Li, Little Li! Listen to what the Party is saying. Toughen yourself; make yourself into a revolutionary warrior. Think of the people of the world. Think of the burden that has been placed upon your shoulders. What right have we to focus on individual pleasures, to think of individual profits and losses?

Little Li is torn between her quest for revolutionary purity and her sense of guilt over her family background:

November 28, 1965

I was born into a family of clerks. Father's and Mother's bourgeois thinking has sunk its roots into my skull. These things come through in our daily conversations and are reinforced in our behavior. I must learn from Hailin and her family so that I can uproot my capitalist ideas and replace them with proletarian thought.

When it comes to competing for a position in the CYL, however, Little Li's idealism gives way to self-interest. She cannot hide her resentment of politically favored classmates:

December 5, 1965

Everyone's all excited because they are going to choose a new CY member from my homeroom. But a new problem has emerged. A few students from revolutionary families have been displaying a sense of superiority, looking down upon their classmates, especially those from ordinary homes.

December 6, 1955

The lucky candidate has been announced.

Zhang Liying, the new CY initiate, comes from a proletarian family background. There is no way I can compare with her.

Even if she cannot disown her family, Little Li can mold herself in the image of revolutionary exemplars lionized in nationwide propaganda campaigns:

December 7, 1955

The reason we study heroes is not so we can become famous and strive to become heroes. We study heroes so that we can better serve the people, so we can act as obedient beasts of burden for the people.

As she approaches her fifteenth birthday, Little Li is not focused on gifts and cake:

December 25, 1965

All kinds of complicated emotions well up in my heart. I am both excited and ashamed. This is no ordinary birthday. It is the first step of my Life as a full-fledged member of the younger generation. Shouldn't I make the most of it? But I don't want (1) anything special to eat and (2) any presents. I want nothing but criticism and self-criticism.

Fifteen years—especially since I entered middle school. I have learned quite a few things. I have studied Mao's Selected Works, a lamp has been lit in my heart, my eyes have become brighter—but my progress has been too slow, my vision has not expanded. I am a person of many words but few deeds.

January 1, 1966

Little Li greets a New Year:

The great year 1966 has arrived. This year marks the beginning of the Third Five Year Plan. Under the leadership of the Party, basking in the brilliant Light of Mao Zedong Thought, the people of the entire nation have been energized and are surging forward, studying [China's model industry] Daqing, practicing [China's model commune] Dazhai, preparing for a monumental victory.

In the past year we have achieved much. We have increased our production of grain, cotton, petroleum, and manufactures and have realized great reforms in culture and science. Domestically we have seen growing prosperity; internationally we view a positive panorama.

In South Vietnam, the People's Liberation Army and the Vietnamese people have already liberated 80 percent of the land. They have smashed the American imperialists to smithereens. In Africa, Latin America, in the very heartland of American imperialism, the fires of the anti-American resistance are burning bright. Confronting these fierce flames, the American imperialists are trembling in their boots! They are scared to death!

In this global upheaval, with the entire world undergoing dynamic change, in this time of great divisions, how can one not be overjoyed to be a Chinese, to be a youth in the Mao Zedong Era? What could be more exciting? I must redouble

my efforts to raise my ideological consciousness, to study hard, and to end the
semester with a smashing victory!

January 15, 1956

*Little Li has been feeling pretty good about her performance on final exams.
But self-esteem has its usual short shelf life:*

I was thinking that missing one question—fourteen points—was no big deal.
But when you are working for your unit and you miss a question, and you let an
enemy escape, is that no big deal? Think about it. When you're at your unit, and
doing Party work, and you miss one question, if you're an engineer, that means
that your entire project comes crashing down on your head.

*After reading some short stories about lives of the proletariat, Little Li
concludes:*

Isn't the new society terrific! Life in the new society is really so happy! People
who say that the new society is inferior to the old are just a bunch of "cow ghosts
and snake demons."

For Little Li, even a family visit is a political event:

January 22, 1956

Today our cousin came over and took us for a stroll. I never imagined he would
buy us a plaster statue of Chairman Mao. I was so happy I broke out in a big grin.
   Now we will have a statue of Mao installed in our dormitory. Every day we
will see the statue of Chairman Mao—just like seeing Mao himself on a daily
basis, as if Chairman Mao was right by our side. One look at him and all our
trials and tribulations dissolve into nothing, one look at him and our hearts are
forever bright.
   Chairman Mao, Chairman Mao, I will follow you forever, I will always obey
you, I will always follow your commands.

January 23, 1956

In my cousin's home we talked about political issues. My cousin's husband
asked me why one should study the thought of Chairman Mao. Why would one
want to join the CYL? What was Marxist-Leninist thought? What was Mao
Zedong thought? My response was tongue-tied silence. . . .

*Taken at face value, these words reveal the shallowness of students' under-
standing of the ideological nostrums they recited every day. But they may*

also show a schoolgirl's reluctance to engage in a dialogue of equals with an older/married cousin.

Here I am at age fifteen. What have I done for the Party and the Motherland? I have studied The Works of Chairman Mao, but I don't know what The Thought of Mao is all about. How can I really learn Maothought? These are the questions confronting me. They await my answer.

January 26, 1956

Little Li's mother asked her what she'd like for her belated birthday dinner. She chose jiaozi—dumplings. So her mother went and borrowed enough money to lay on a jiaozi feast. But instead of praising her mother's thought-fulness, the puritanical fifteen-year-old tells her diary what a terrible thing it is to indulge in such luxuries when they could get along on simpler fare. A birthday party has become a betrayal of the Communist Party. Shame! Shame!

January 27, 1956

Little Li's blessing (or is it her curse?) is her ability to link personal life with political ideals on all occasions—even while competing in a track meet:

Racing through my mind: "One lap, two laps, three laps. I was already a Little short of breath, my legs were feeling heavier, I wanted to slow down. I was barely managing to keep up. My mind was waging an arduous struggle. Could I run the last four laps? Could I keep it up? While running, I thought of the Red Army and the People's Liberation Army. For the revolution, for the Liberation of China, they ran their hearts out, more than a hundred Li a day. Are you telling me they didn't get tired? Tired! But for the revolution, for us, they ran and ran and ran, pursuing, pursuing, ever pursuing the enemy, wiping out the enemy.

Now it was me running, and I was also chasing down the enemy, chasing down the American imperialist invaders of Vietnam, helping the people of Vietnam. I must keep up, have to keep up with them. I have made a commit-ment; I will absolutely keep up with them. Step by step I was gaining on them. The last lap. I was on the final lap. Now I'm going to catch up. I was keeping up, slowly catching up, but I didn't slow down. I would keep up, keep up. In the end, though I didn't catch them, my heart was filled with joy. I had finally moved a step ahead.

February 2, 1956

Feb. 2, first day of the spring semester. School official gives a talk. The emphasis this semester will be on the living application of The Thoughts of Chairman Mao.

Little Li plans to spend half an hour every Tuesday, Thursday, and Sunday studying Mao's Selected Works—in addition to her morning runs. If she has any energy left, she will study technical things like airplane models, transistor radios, radio repair, and growing vegetables.

In the final analysis, Little Li is trapped by an inexorable contradiction: She has committed herself to living a life for others—for country, for revolution, for her schoolmates, for the peasants—and yet she is inexorably consumed by selfish concerns:

February 4, 1956

Sometimes when I have nothing to do, I feel emotionally empty. I have no energy. I'm Like a wooden statue, totally exhausted. I'm not happy. So I think it over. What's the reason? Why am I so listless? The more I think about it the more I realize that it all comes back to individualism. Whenever there is something going on, whenever I'm talking and laughing with other people, I don't have these feelings. But the moment I'm by myself with nothing to do, all kinds of ideas flood into my mind. When will I get into CY? Why have I not been chosen a squad captain? Why does Pan Xiaowen ignore me like that? These problems tie me in knots. Right now, on the international front, American imperialism is getting more deeply involved in its wars every day and revisionism is stepping forth to help them. In Vietnam the Americans are sending more and more soldiers. And all around our country's borders they are building military bases. The American imperialists have dragged South Korea and Japan into a "Japanese-Korean Treaty." But the more deranged the American imperialists and the reactionary clique becomes the clearer it is that they are moving toward defeat, moving toward obliteration! People of every country are rising up to oppose American imperialism—especially in the American imperialists own lair—the United States itself, where the angry flames of anti-imperialism are also spreading, and all over the world, people are tightening the noose around the American imperialists.

In China, heroes are stepping forward, nurtured by the Thought of Mao Zedong, so many heroes surging forward! All over the country Mao Zedong Thought is sprouting and taking root. A great tide of studying the Works of Chairman Mao is welling up! Doesn't that make you happy? Revolution—what does this age ask of us? When you see these things and you think of the demands of the era, when can you possible feel empty inside? How can you possibly think of yourself? In such an era, in this kind of surging tide, if you don't join the collective ranks, if you don't throw yourself into this sea, you will end up being but an isolated drop of water, totally helpless, destined to dry up in oblivion!

At fifteen, Little Li has few doubts about the meaning of life:

March 1, 1956

Why are you born? Why do you die? You are born for the Party, for the People, for the Revolution and you die for the Party, for the People, for the Revolution.

Preserved through more than half a century of turmoil and upheavals, Little Li's diary reveals what ultimately inspired a teenage girl to leave the comforts of Beijing for a life of hardship in a distant wilderness. Such a resolution would, however, have been impossible without the Great Proletarian Cultural Revolution.

Chapter 3

A Political Tsunami

The charismatic Cult of Chairman Mao. The talismanic Little Red Book. The Cultural Revolution's appeal to middle and high school students eager to transform youthful idealism into revolutionary activism. Looking above for direction, this generation faced a political tsunami.

The Cultural Revolution was announced on May 16, 1966, as a purge of "counter-revolutionary revisionists" who had "sneaked into the Party, the government, the army, and various spheres of culture." Informed that Mao himself was under attack, self-styled "Red Guards" at the Tsinghua High School and other institutions sprang to his defense. Shock waves reverberated through Beijing's secondary schools where the Fifty-fivers were enrolled.

For youngsters growing up in the newly established PRC, political movements were routine. More than once schoolwork had been pushed aside by new slogans, campaigns, crusades, heroes to be emulated, villains to be excoriated. Students were accustomed to classroom exhortations, bulletin board proclamations, slogans blasted from loudspeakers, drills on athletic fields, mass rallies in Tiananmen Square.

Everyone knew what was expected: Take cues from your classroom teacher, school principal, Party secretary. Follow the flag. Internalize the message. Make the right moves. Mouth prescribed slogans. Follow the twists and turns of the movement wherever it might lead. For those in doubt, fake conviction. For true believers, obedience was effortless.

To maintain a semblance of emotional balance, it was best to believe. Doubt could only bring anguish. One could hope to survive, politically and psychologically, if there was no tension between outward behavior and inner conviction.

The Cultural Revolution was different. It could neither be incorporated into academic routines nor hitched to life's trajectories. The new reality became crystal clear when officials announced that China's schools, from kindergartens through universities, were to be shut down—peremptorily and indefinitely.

At No. 65 High School, which catered to the college-bound, the proclamation hit members of the third-year class like a ton of bricks. These young men and women had already completed graduation requirements when they learned that the college entrance exams for which they were ferociously preparing had been canceled. By now they understood that rank-and-file students could no longer remain aloof from the high-level political purge that had already shaken up the Beijing city government and the central propaganda apparatus. At one school after another, students had posted big-character posters that vilified once-revered teachers and administrators as "reactionaries" and [pro-USSR] "revisionists." The elite No. 65 could not remain aloof.

While classmates crammed for college entrance exams, Li Saiyang, a graduating senior just turned twenty, had stood aside because he had more exciting prospects. With the unraveling of fraternal ties with the Soviet Union, China was opening channels outside of Moscow's bloc to gain exposure to the world. As No. 65's sole recipient of a highly coveted scholarship to study in France, Li was undergoing orientation at the Ministry of Foreign Affairs.

Parisian reveries shattered, Li now returned to his campus to plunge into the burgeoning Cultural Revolution. As the son of officials, however, there was no way that he could align himself with the "rebels" who attacked the Communist Party–controlled political structure in the name of revolutionary virtue. A scion of Beijing's political establishment could scarcely think of smashing his own rice bowl.

Scripting his school's very first big character poster, Li declared "that we will defend to the death the Party's absolute leadership of the Cultural Revolution." That he had chosen the wrong side became evident when Mao Zedong wrote his own poster titled "Bombard the Headquarters," prodding students to redirect revolutionary passions against the Party establishment. The result, Li ruefully recalled, was that "I turned overnight from a model student to a budding revisionist."

No sooner had the semester ended than Li and other graduating seniors found themselves confronting an existential crisis: To cling to old dreams of college and career would bring self-immolation in the fires of revolution. Within a fortnight, two edicts proclaimed the new reality—a June 1 announcement that Beijing's schools and universities would immediately be closed and a June 13 sequel extending the edict to the rest of China.

Some half of those whose names would appear on the roster of the Beijing Fifty-five—nineteen of the thirty-one boys and eight of the twenty-four girls—had just completed their third year of high school. These young men and women faced a dark future. An Zhenke's dream had evaporated:

> I was preparing to study the humanities in college. That was my strength, especially language and literature and foreign language. I was already learning

Russian. In June 1966 the Cultural Revolution began and all academic activities came to an abrupt halt, as did our review for the university entrance examination. After that, the rebel faction in our school rose up and began a struggle for power. The academic climate simply went up in smoke.

Interviewed three decades later, many Fifty-fivers echoed An's angst. One, however, shared very different memories. Wang Xiaoyun was not part of the college-bound elite but simply an ordinary student at an average school. Here is what she recalled:

With the termination of the university entrance exams, we all lost our chance to receive a higher education, which we should feel as a negative thing. But at that time, we felt a sort of personal transformation, something new though it was hard to put into words, anyway something very exciting. . . . We felt no sadness, no disappointment. We felt a sense of something new and fresh.

In contrast, Li Saiyang and fellow high school graduates found the dashing of youthful dreams and aspirations as anything but "new and fresh":

Teachers and administrators targeted by Red Guards witnessed the institutions where they had achieved recognition as symbols of knowledge and authority transformed into sites of a brutal inquisition. At Peng Zhenge's school, during "Criticism and Struggle Meetings," students used military belts to whip the Director of Instruction. They issued a command that the woman who taught biology have her head shaven. Teachers undergoing criticism had to return to the school daily to clean toilets. As they lined up for work, the Red Guards made them sing the "Cow Devil Snake Spirit" song: "I am a Cow Devil Snake Spirit. I am an enemy of the people. I am guilty. I deserve to die. I am guilty. I deserve to die." The Communist Youth League Secretary also had his head shaven.

Red Guard terrorists brazenly marched into homes, destroying photos, works of art, and phonograph records, subjecting occupants to verbal harassment and physical abuse, sometimes beating people to death. Though none of the Fifty-fivers admits involvement in such activities, all were aware of what was going on.

Even youngsters who championed Chairman Mao's revolutionary critique of the establishment could not save families from persecution at the hands of vengeful Red Guards. Su Baikai, another member of No. 25 High School's graduating class, had been raised in a household of intellectuals loosely affiliated with the old order. Though his family lacked the official connections of Li Saiyang, Su's father had endowed him with a commitment to the ideals of a new China. Su recalled his big character poster—the first at his school— echoing the Maoist critique of the educational order, lambasting China's schools as narrowly academic, elitist, "expert-and-not-red—the whole revisionist syndrome."

Despite sterling academic credentials and organizational skills, Su had nonetheless been denied admission to CYL because of his family background. However politically correct his big character poster, his home, with its pre-revolutionary lifestyle, was an inviting target for the Red Guard interrogation and confiscation gang that marched through the front door and turned the family's living room into a chamber of hell:

> In a single evening I was changed from a Little Revolutionary General to a target of the revolution. . . . There we were lined up like the landlords used to be, all in a row, everyone bending their heads. Of course I was not personally in this line. They were my dad's generation, all of them lowered heads and bent waists, subjecting themselves to criticism, with nowhere to turn for help. I was filled with righteous indignation, absolutely livid. I wanted to run out and get reinforcements. I myself wasn't a regular Red Guard but there were some old Red Guards among my fellow students, and I thought of getting them over. We wouldn't have to get into a fight with those guys but at least we could talk reason, make everything clear—but my uncle stopped me in my tracks.
>
>   After undergoing this kind of experience, I thought long and hard about the Red Guards. Of course I hadn't been an actual member. But I really felt they had been used by [Mao's wife] Jiang Qing and the Gang of Four. They were filled with revolutionary fanaticism, but they didn't know a damned thing.

Even tried and trusted bulwarks of revolutionary order such as the CYL provided no security for Beijing's aspiring political and intellectual elite. Chen Jinsheng, Su's fellow student at No. 25 High School, was one of a coterie of upended seniors:

> We felt that things couldn't go on like this. With nobody in charge, we were extremely apprehensive—because we were about to graduate. If no one took care of us, how could we take the college entrance exams? That's the way we felt! So we were really upset. We personally went to the CYL Central Committee and asked them to send a work team to manage our school.

Appeals to higher authority backfired:

> After we had welcomed them in, the work team turned and rectified us. You see, we had organized a small coterie, the "East Wind Group." We could evaluate our teachers, form an attack team. They said, "How dare you organize this kind of outfit? Such things are illegal." We said, "No way; according to the Constitution, they're legal." The work team went through our dossier. . . . They rectified us up and down, labeled us a counter-revolutionary cabal. We had to criticize ourselves. After that they singled out several people in our class as "evil

bosses." And we all became targets. We were supposed to criticize our own fellow students. We had to criticize our own leaders, the leaders of our East Wind organization. . . . What a joke!

No matter which way young people turned, they found no way out. Even a casual stroll could unveil a tableau of horror. Peng Zhenge:

> As I was walking past the 21st High School, I spotted a large van from the mortuary parked on the corner. Lots of kids were climbing on board to see what was inside. I also hopped on. What I saw was a pile of corpses collected from various high schools. Suddenly I saw a bunch of stretcher-bearers carrying out corpses from the 21st High School, chasing away sightseers as they went. After throwing the corpses into the truck, they seated themselves on the two sides and, without the slightest sign of emotion, took off.

A defining moment in the Cultural Revolution came on August 18, the first of eight Red Guard rallies in Tiananmen Square presided over by the "Great Leader/Great Teacher/Great Commander/Great Helmsman" Mao Zedong. Here the Chairman gave his blessings to the "revolutionary" acts of his "little generals." With Mao's blessings, young fanatics now embarked upon a two-month-long reign of terror against people, edifices, and artifacts deemed representative of the "Four Olds"—Old Ideas, Old Culture, Old Habits, and Old Customs.

To extricate himself from the culture of violence while remaining politically correct, Li Saiyang, like many others, joined a group of fellow students to travel around China observing current conditions and visiting revolutionary sites. "We walked all the way to Yan'an," recalled Li. "We underwent all kinds of hardships and gained insights into Chinese society."

These expeditions burgeoned into a nationwide "Movement to Exchange Revolutionary Experiences"—*chuanlian.*

Chuanlian was a godsend for youth whose appetites for raising hell in their own schools and municipalities had already been sated but who had little stomach for terrorism. Literally meaning "to disseminate and link up," the *chuanlian* rubric enabled groups of youngsters—whether or not Red Guards—to explore China's vast landscape, with transportation, room, and board provided by the state. Though the official rationale was to promote a nationwide crusade against "authorities in power following the capitalist road," political considerations aside, this opportunity to explore the fabled realms of their motherland was too good to pass up. Not by chance has *chuanlian* been labeled "revolutionary tourism."

By the end of 1966 and the beginning of 1967 *chuanlian* had taken its toll on China's bureaucratic order and the rail system—to say nothing of the national exchequer. Officials responded with a series of edicts: No more *chuanlian*! Come home! Now!

Young pilgrims dutifully obeyed. However, with the Cultural Revolution still in progress, issues of governance and political power highly contested, and millions of Red Guards prepared to march to the barricades of revolution, larger problems remained. Instructed to restore discipline, units of the PLA descended upon high school campuses to bring students in line with the new policy: *Fuke Naogeming*—"Return to Class and Make Revolution." Under the watchful eyes of the armed forces, however, there were severe limits on how much "revolution" anybody would be permitted to make.

The new slogan, moreover, failed to address an existential dilemma. Many Beijing middle and high school students, especially the older and more thoughtful, had had their fill of *revolution* and would have been perfectly happy to resume education. But even though school doors were open, study remained in limbo. Academic activities, recalls Lin Ni, were a bad joke:

> Under the guidance of military propaganda squads, Beijing's middle and high schools were starting to "Return to Class and Make Revolution"—physical education was replaced by military training, study of "The Sayings of Chairman Mao" replaced mathematics, physics, and chemistry—school was hopeless, employment impossible.

With learning in limbo and political activism sharply constrained, a vacuum filled the lives of Beijing students. For many, however, and quite certainly for most of those who would sign up for the Yunnan expedition, what was needed was a way to guide political passions into constructive channels.

Returning to Beijing from his *chuanlian* adventures, an Establishment Faction stalwart did what he could to mitigate the destructiveness of Red Guard radicals. When violence erupted, Li Saiyang

> worked to bring things under control. Our school's Party Secretary had been beaten to within an inch of his life by students from some high school. We carried him off in a pedicab cart and saved his life.

But there were limits on what young Li and his confederates could do:

> I didn't go around organizing as some people did and there was no way I could have done so at that time. I simply didn't see eye to eye with the way things were being handled.

A prominent member of Li's graduating class was He Longkang, son of a prominent official and himself a CYL activist. Turned off by Red Guard vigilantes who pillaged family treasures, He and his friends took pains to identify things of cultural value that should be protected and did our best to save them. We went so far as to argue that such activities shouldn't be given free reign—and even to inject a bit of humanity into the whole enterprise.

Whatever China's problems, He, like fellow moderates, now understood that constructive solutions were imperative:

After the campaign against the "Four Olds" had run its course in the late summer and early fall of 1966, we gradually cooled down and realized that raising hell wasn't the answer. . . . It was then that we began to consider what path we should take going forward. . . . We finally reached the conclusion that we would no longer participate in the so-called Cultural Revolution, which would only give us more headaches. . . . The new mantra was to "throw yourself into industrial and agricultural production."

There were, in fact, two radically different ways of understanding this notion. Chairman Mao's idea was for us to submit ourselves to reeducation at the hands of the poor and lower-middle peasants. Seen from a political perspective, this was one option.

Then there was Zhou Enlai's construction—promoting the development of production. . . . At that time we felt we had enormous abilities, that we were prepared to undertake a very important historical mission.

Those hoping to blaze a new trail had to begin within the confines of their demoralized schools. Happily, just as the *Fuke Naogeming* slogan was wearing thin, another came to the rescue: *Dou-Pi-Gai*—Struggle-Criticism-Transformation. The beauty of this formulation was precisely in its vagueness. "Struggle" captured the militancy and moral energy that had made the Cultural Revolution an explosive force. "Criticism" implied the use of reason and logic to weed out incorrect and outmoded ideas—an analytic process attractive to budding intellectuals. "Transformation" offered hope for a brighter future that would do away with the irrationalities and inequities of the past. Under the organizational umbrella of the Beijing Red Guard Congress, the Eastern district schools organized a Red Guard Congress Struggle/Criticism/Transformation Office. At the point, He Longkang testifies:

We proposed returning to classes to make revolution, working through the Dou-Pi-Gai model. Struggle was the struggle against capitalist roaders; Criticism was criticism of incorrect ideas, capitalist ideas; Transformation was to transform the old educational system and to create a new one. . . . All the schools had *Dou-Pi-Gai* offices but our 65th High provided a focal point for the others for organization, research, investigation, and analysis.

No. 65 was situated in Beijing's Eastern District. Here, the local Red Guards Congress formed its own Struggle-Criticism-Transformation Office to channel student energies into constructive projects. An exhibit on Chinese education since the founding of the PRC recruited youngsters turned off by a Red Guard movement fractured by ideological rifts, clique loyalties, and political opportunism.

Divisive factionalism, however, continued to turn students against each other. Based upon remarks that Mao's wife, Jiang Qing, had made at meetings on consecutive days, high school students aligned themselves in the April 3 and April 4 cliques. You Hai recalled:

> At the outset I was an April 3rd. The April 4's were also on the scene. Fights broke out between the two. I was exhausted by all this. Whatever the issue, the 3s would say this, the 4s that. Everyone wanted to promote their own point of view.

Dou-Pi-Gai provided a cover for diverse initiatives. While some focused upon educational reform, others encouraged students to seek new frontiers beyond the world of schools and books on "the front lines of industrial and agricultural production." Seeking bureaucratic support for such a project, He Longkang reached out to the Agricultural Reclamation Ministry. You Hai too was anxious to test newly honed political and organizational skills in a more challenging setting:

> I was fed up with all this bickering about which line was revolutionary, which reactionary. If we were going to have an exhibit, everyone would have to get to work. Since everyone is fighting against each other over endless issues and nobody else was doing it, I took it upon myself. I pasted things up, I sawed the characters, I mixed the paste. So everyone liked me. Everyone wanted to have their photos taken with me. They treated me well. Some *4.3s* said, I was a turn-coat, but I got along fine with most everyone. It was then that I began to feel that politics was boring and pointless. It was then that I began to think about going to the frontier. Then let them see who was really revolutionary and who was a phony revolutionary by tempering their souls in the furnace of revolution!

Others returning from "exchanging revolutionary experiences" found themselves with time on their hands. For many, exhortations to "Return to Class and Make Revolution" rang hollow. The old academic routine had been shattered, and, for those who had just completed their final year of high school, there were no classes left to take.

At No. 65 High, where budding leaders such as He Longkang and Li Saiyang were seeking a political strategy that would live up to the revolutionary standards of Chairman Mao without unleashing a nihilist assault on the establishment that they aspired to join, other students invented creative ways to mark time. Yan Si recalls:

We would go to school in the morning, find an empty room, set up a table, and play poker until lunchtime. Then we'd go back to the poker game. We set up a mirror next to the door so that we could see if anyone was coming. If the representative from the work team or the army approached, we'd hide the cards and take out our *Selections from the Works of Mao Zedong.*

During the summer of 1966, while gangs of Red Guards turned to ever more violent forms of revolutionary activism, these disillusioned revolutionary dropouts were perfecting the fine art of fence-sitting. For youngsters seeking a new path, an opportunity to prove themselves on China's borderland offered an alluring alternative to a life of cynicism and boredom.

Chapter 4

From Beijing to Banna

"Unite with the workers and peasants!"—the slogan reverberated in the ears of urban students seeking a path out of the Cultural Revolutionary morass. Mao famously defined the distinction between truly revolutionary intellectuals and mere pretenders as whether or not they joined forces with the toiling masses. With time on their hands and prospects for the future dashed, more than a few young Beijingers now saw hope for redemption through hard labor in fields, factories, and mines. No. 5 High student Zhang Xinhui, who spent several months working a lathe, recalled:

> How can I put it? It was a kind of way, a kind of idea. . . . It wasn't a way to make a living. But we had to find something to do, some way to steel ourselves, to learn to do something.

Having completed only the first of their three-year curriculum at No. 5 High and having returned from a tour to "exchange revolutionary experiences," Sun Ling and Yin Zheng went to work in the Beijing Motor Vehicle Factory. Fueled by youthful energy and eager to flaunt proletarian ideals, the youngsters threw themselves into their jobs even after fellow employees let them know in no uncertain terms that the factory's accustomed work ethic was considerably more leisurely. As Sun recalled:

> Back then the workers—including our supervisor—were all moonlighting on company time. Nobody paid any attention to them. Yin and I were working our tails off, like earnest apprentices . . . trying to outdo each other.

One of No. 65 High's frustrated graduating seniors—He Longkang—cast his eyes further afield:

> By November '66, the high tide of the first phase of the Cultural Revolution—rebelling and exchanging revolutionary experiences—had passed and the second—Struggle/Criticize/Transform—was gradually starting. With college

doors closed, the issue was what to do, where to go. To get a handle on the situation, the Red Guards Union, Old Red Guards, and other students of the 65th got together on their own initiative and started knocking on government office doors.

An official at the National Agricultural Reclamation Ministry informed them that rubber was a national strategic resource, one of China's four basic raw materials. Xishuangbanna, like Hainan, enjoyed favorable conditions for rubber culture and was in the process of becoming the country's number two production base. The Ministry therefore agreed to make connections for us to go to Yunnan to assess the situation and provided us with appropriate official introductions. In late 1966, five students from the 65th High launched an exploratory expedition to Yunnan.

The decision to head for China's tropical frontier was driven not only by patriotic zeal to make China self-sufficient in rubber production, but also, as He Longkang later admitted, by opportunism:

> Though a lifelong Beijing resident, I had always detested the cold climate. Since it was all in the same revolutionary cause, why would I want to set out for the icy Northeast or Inner Mongolia when I could go to balmy Yunnan? Quite clearly, even in that era, revolutionary slogans could not totally crowd out individual aspirations and, amidst heroic declamations, there was still room for a wee bit of individualistic calculation.

Disembarking from the train in Yunnan's capital, Kunming, delegates were greeted by a factotum assigned to receive visiting young revolutionaries. The official found himself challenged, however, not by the customary delegation of Red Guard activists and revolutionary tourists but by a group of volunteers for rural labor. He hastened to introduce the intrepid volunteers to the head of the political office of the Provincial Department of Agriculture and Forestry, who passed them down to the Yunnan Rubber Reclamation Project in Xishuangbanna.

A four-day drive over primitive roads took the young pioneers to Banna's capital, Jinghong, from which local officials escorted them through the tropical forests to potential sites for rubber plantations. Everywhere they went the red carpet was rolled out. In Jinghong, they were quartered on the banks of the majestic Mekong at the Prefectural Government Guesthouse where Premier Zhou Enlai had stayed on a recent visit. In off-hours, they hiked mountain trails, played basketball with farm workers, and staged performances in league with the Jinghong Farm Propaganda Corps. After Xishuangbanna's mountain highs, however, going back to Kunming was a sobering experience:

The Cultural Revolution had taken a turn for the worse and rebellions and struggles for power were reaching the boiling point. Provincial officials were no longer in a position to look after us, and the official channel to Yunnan that we had so assiduously cultivated was cut off. Our project temporarily ground to a halt.

Back in Beijing, however, they pressed on. From their headquarters in the Struggle/Criticism/Transfomation Office of the East Beijing Red Guards Congress, high school activists solicited recruits. Frustrated by the grotesque turns of the Cultural Revolution and driven by idealistic zeal, volunteers showed up in a dozen middle and high schools. New converts included Su Baikai, a gregarious extrovert with dazzling organizational skills and a magnetic personality. You Hai recalls the passion that drew her into the group:

For a seventeen-year-old girl to want to join a bunch of people she didn't even know and run off to Yunnan shows that my "revolutionary" consciousness had reached the point of insanity.

For others, the life-changing decision was quite random. One ran into an acquaintance while descending a flight of stairs. When his friend asked if he was going to Yunnan, he instantly responded, "I'm going." And that was it. But, recalls Peng Zhenge, individual choices sometimes intersected with larger events:

Just when I was waiting for permission to work at a military industry—that was with Wang Kaiping who had also decided not to take the college entrance exams—Qu Zhe organized the first group of *zhiqing* volunteers, a few dozen students determined to go to the villages of Inner Mongolia. Subsequently the first group left for Heilongjiang, several hundred students I believe. That was the day Wang Kaiping told me they were planning to go to Banna. On the spur of the moment, I said to him, "Actually, I'd like very much to go with you." Several good friends who overheard me gathered round and said, "If you go, so will we!" That's how I made my decision to go. And it was clear that the others who had spent three years in high school and two in the Cultural Revolution were also solidly committed. There were five of us.

You Hai discovered that winning acceptance as a member of the Yunnan expedition was anything but a foregone conclusion:

Besides being totally clueless, I also had to pass a rigorous cross-examination at the hands of some of the organizers who were just a bit older than me. The approval process was more drawn out than for any job I have applied for since moving to the States.

One cold winter's evening I walked into a spacious room in no. 8 Coal Dust Alley. In front of me, gathered round a large cast iron heater, were three people, two sitting, one standing. The standing one, in an army overcoat, stood tall and straight, with a sharp hawk-like nose. The formal interview involved the three taking turns interrogating me, while I nervously and meticulously answered each one:

"Everything is very tough there. We'll have to provide for ourselves. We might have to live under a big tree."

That kind of question was music to my ears. In a high state of excitement, I replied: "The tougher it is, the more revolutionary." No way such an answer could disappoint.

"There will be malaria, wild animals, snakes . . . "

Malaria. I hadn't a clue what that was all about. When he said "snakes," my heart skipped a beat. I had always been scared of snakes. Once in primary school, a naughty little boy had dangled a caterpillar against the back of my neck and I had cried for a week. But after an instant's hesitation, I shot right back, "If you're not afraid of them, neither am I." My voice may have betrayed some lack of conviction, but I don't think I lost too many points.

By the time the day for approval arrived, I was beside myself with anxiety. For the life of me I can't understand why they took something that was so easy for everyone else and made it such an ordeal for me.

Years later, with the benefit of hindsight, You Hai reflected on how nearly her clique affiliations had caused her to be blackballed:

Among my interrogators, Su Baikai was a *4.4*, as was his friend Wang. Later Wu Sibing said that if he had known I was a *4.3* he absolutely would have rejected me.

Even with ranks swelled by new recruits, the Yunnan expedition was anything but a done deal—as He Longkang recalls:

By the second half of 1967 our Yunnan contacts were still cut off. Everyone felt we couldn't go on like this, so they decided to send a second delegation. By then *Exchanging Revolutionary Experiences* had already ended and you could no longer ride the rails for free. So, we took up a collection. In October 1967 four of us set out for Kunming.

What met them on arrival was not encouraging. Rent by armed struggle, Yunnan had been placed under military rule. Local officials could only send them back to Beijing with advice to seek support from city or central government authorities. At the Kunming train station, the four found themselves in dire straits:

Our cash had run out and we didn't even have enough for return train tickets. So, we bought tickets to Shuicheng in Guizhou, one of the earlier stops on the long-distance train with the intention of trying our luck once we were on board. Beyond that station, we hid under the seats to avoid confronting the conductor. Finally, we realized we couldn't go on like this, so we went and explained the situation to the conductor and did what we could to ingratiate ourselves and make ourselves—cleaning the cars, performing songs for the passengers. Our repertoire included the famous Cultural Revolutionary ballad, "Our Generation." The campaign worked—and we arrived home safely.

Sobered by their abortive expedition, they now realized that, in the absence of official support, even the most zealous recruitment crusade would lead to nothing. So,

braving the bitter winter winds, we hopped on our bikes and headed over to the Beijing Revolutionary Committee and the Beijing City Arrangements Office. But we always got the same answer: Beijing had made no arrangements for sending people to Yunnan and there was no way to link up with Yunnan.

How to break the impasse? The answer comes from Lin Ni:

While groping around, a few students, especially those in high schools, began to ask the question: What's the next step? Where are we headed?

Activists in the Dou-Pi-Gai office assessed the situation:

Issue number 1: How to resolve the question of what future lay ahead for our six grades of middle and high school students. To see it described in the newspapers, it could be said that we enjoyed an "excellent overall revolutionary situation." The facts were that government institutions were paralyzed, factories unproductive, schools shuttered. Only the peasants were, as usual, carrying out the mission of the "revolutionary masses"—to provide enough grain to feed the nation. And among the recently graduated 3rd year high school and 3rd year middle school students, only a minute fraction from "good" family backgrounds could join the army or get a job in rear area defense industries. Confronting Central authorities was an unresolved issue: How to employ the vast majority of students?

Issue number 2: How were we expected to realize our assigned role as China's putative "revolutionary successors"? Whether or not scions of "good, solid" families, all students of that era considered themselves "sons and daughters of the New China, raised under the Red Flag." In our hearts, all of us had "unlimited love, unlimited respect" for Chairman Mao. All cherished high aspirations and shining ideals, all were committed to giving everything for the Socialist Motherland and the Human Race. Our thinking and mental explorations all led to a common conclusion: In the process of striding forward on the path of unity with the workers and peasants, we would discover life's realities by struggling through the storm to plunge into China's vast expanse of rural villages, reconstructing our own subjective worlds even as we reconstructed the objective world, thereby forging ourselves into the true revolutionary successors of the great enterprise that was the Proletarian Revolution.

This kind of commitment is what we were all about. It stemmed from a true and sincere *weltanschauung* that identified us with the larger world around us, a spirit of youthful resolve, a profoundly idealistic ethos—we viewed our individual choices with pride, with excitement, and not without a certain degree of self-appreciation.

Looking back after the passage of several decades, we see something of which we could not have been conscious at the time, namely the contradiction and perplexities that stood between the "excellent overall situation" and the sordid reality, the chasm that separated revolutionary heroics and fanaticism from the depression that came once we were beaten down. (No small number of people found friends and relatives transformed overnight from the driving force of revolution to targets of revolution, objects of struggle and confinement.) So quite a few discovered themselves, quite inadvertently, searching for a way to escape from the realities that hemmed them in.

To enter a new world and transform it, energize the lives of its people, and at the same time achieve self-realization—these were our goals. Chaos and oppression had already destroyed any sense of attachment that people might have had for big city life.

Zhou Enlai Approves!

For all their success in peer recruitment, organizers of the Yunnan expedition had yet to break through the official impasse:

> We had tried everything. It looked hopeless. But our spirit was tenacious. At that time the Chinese people had a pattern of behavior—whenever you encounter an intractable problem, go straight to the Central Authorities—and the only Central Authority we hadn't gotten to was the Premier! He would surely understand us and help us. So we had drafted a report which put into words our hot-blooded passion. But all that counted for naught if we couldn't find an opportunity to present it to Premier Zhou Enlai.
>
> Suddenly one day I received the same news from two different sources. Both phoned to say that the Premier was conferring with industry and trade representatives—and it was possible for us to gain admission to the meeting hall. All of a sudden we had our opening. I scooped up two of our group who happened to be in the office—Zhang Cunlong and Zhang Xinhui—and the three of us ran over to the Great Hall of the People. We entered the Hunan Hall, where we found the Premier listening to reports.
>
> At that moment we realized that, in our haste, we had left behind our petition to the Premier! No time to go back and get it. We'd have to draft another on the

spot. But we couldn't find a proper sheet of paper. I'd have to dictate it from memory. Zhang Xinhui would fill in any blanks, and Zhang Cunlong would write it down. On a ragged scrap of paper, we wrote out the memo that would determine our fate. It was headed "A Petition from Middle and High School Students in the Nation's Capital Seeking Permission to Go to Yunnan."

Having hastily written out our appeal, we now watched for a chance to deliver it to the Premier. Time was flying. Suddenly, we saw [Vice-Premier] Li Xiannian get up and move toward the exit. Was the meeting over then? Our hearts sank. If we had missed our chance, we were finished, kaput. We scurried toward the exit, hoping that we could present it to him on his way out. But after a few minutes, Li Xiannian came back. He had only gone to the restroom. Though it had been a false alarm, we were nervous as hell. We dared not relax even for a minute. A little while later—I have no idea exactly how long it was—the Premier got up and left the hall. The three of us rushed to the doorway to wait for him to come back.

Before long the Premier returned from the restroom. We instantly accosted him. Finding ourselves standing in front of that tired but compassionate face, we were bathed in a sense of warmth. Our nervousness had miraculously disappeared. In way of self-introduction, I said to the Premier: "We are high school Red Guards. We want to go to the Yunnan border to make our contribution to building up the borderland and turning it into the nation's number two natural rubber base." The Premier looked us over and inquired: "Haven't you returned to school to make revolution?" We replied, "Classes have already resumed, and the Military Propaganda Squad is stationed at our school, but we are recent third year graduates of middle and high schools. We want to get started making our contribution to Chinese society as soon as possible."

As we were talking, we handed the Premier that little piece of paper containing the hopes and dreams of a bunch of eighteen-year-old youths. We were so nervous and excited that we couldn't hear our own voices. I don't remember exactly what I said. All I recall is the Premier saying "OK, I'll take a look at your petition!" Then, holding our dreams in his hand, he returned to his seat. From this instant, a sense of uneasiness and all kinds of conjectures replaced our heroic resolve and sense of excitement. Standing in the last row of the meeting place, we dared not sit down. We just remained standing on tiptoes looking ahead. What we saw was the Premier focusing his attention on that little piece of paper. Then he wrote something on it. Even though we did everything we could to figure out what the Premier was up to, there was no way we could guess what he had written.

By the time we got back, it was already dark but nobody had gone home. They were all waiting to debrief us. The three of us related our experience in minute detail, including the Premier's every move, every gesture, but we told them there was no way we could deduce what the Premier had written on that piece of paper. Was it "Yes" or "No"? Everything was a mystery.

One thing, however, was clear: with the administrative organs of the entire country in a state of paralysis, life and death issues facing a country of eight hundred million people rested on the split-second decisions of a single man. Faced with "SOS" calls from every corner of the land, the overheated emotions of the rebel faction, the nefarious dealings of "Auntie Jiang Qing" [Mme Mao Zedong], the Premier didn't even have time to eat and sleep. But he had given such a warm and generous hearing to a bunch of wet-behind-the-ears high school students, so patiently heard us out, engaged us in dialogue. . . . Whether or not he was able to grant our request, the Premier would certainly manage to make everything come out OK, just as our parents would. So we sat there waiting, hoping. Each day was like a year.

He Longkang picks up the story:

Several days later a representative of the Planning Office of the Beijing City Revolutionary Committee received our representatives, told us that Premier Zhou had agreed to our request, and showed us his signed approval. We saw his pencil-written note on our report: "Comrades Fuchun and Qiuli: We can give positive consideration to this request. Please coordinate with the Beijing City Revolutionary Committee.—Zhou Enlai." Concrete authorization was given by Vice-Premier Li Fuchun and by Ding Guoyu and Niu Lianbi of the Beijing City Revolutionary Committee, directing Comrade Gao Hansong of the City Revolutionary Committee's Planning Office to connect with Yunnan. This document was designated 1967 Document no. 6770.

Our efforts had paid off and a heavy rock was lifted from our hearts.

Figure 4.1. Mentougou Coal Mine. (Chen Xinzeng collection)

While waiting for Beijing leaders to connect with Yunnan, expedition organizers geared up for the trip:

> In addition to each individual packing luggage and getting ready in a physical sense, we had to prepare ourselves mentally. On December 25, 1967, our entire group went to the People's Palace of Culture to see the "Bethune Exhibit" to inspire ourselves with the spirit of Norman Bethune [a Canadian Communist volunteer martyred during the Anti-Japanese War].
>
> To get in shape for the rigorous life ahead, from December 31, 1967, to January 23, 1968, our entire group went to the Mentougou Coal Mine west of the city for nearly a month of labor and indoctrination [see Figure 4.1]. Together with the workers, we went to work in the mine, riding the cable car down, then switching to the mining cart, and finally walking to the face of the seam of coal. We learned to drill holes, set charges, and to shovel up coal to send to the surface. We put in eight-hour days. When you added the time it took getting back to the surface and washing up, each working day was more than ten hours. In addition, we studied and conferred with the PLA. . . . During this period, the mine set a daily production record of 5037.3 tons, thanks in part to our contribution.

For teenage school kids, the month in the mine was a trial by fire. Driven by China's socialist and feminist ideals, the girls outdid themselves to prove that "Women Hold Up Half the Sky" was more than an empty slogan. Before they arrived, women mine workers had only been allowed to work machines. Now, for the first time, members of both sexes attacked the mine face with picks and shovels. Students left the Mentougou mine strengthened by a respect for the contribution of female classmates, a sense of self-esteem, and an ethos of group solidarity.

Though great for physical toughening, psychological conditioning, and social bonding, the mining venture taught students nothing about rubber production. Fortuitously, Peng Zhenge's father had actually managed a rubber plantation on Hainan Island. Peng and his comrades lost no opportunity to draw upon the elder Peng's experience:

> He related the history of how overseas Chinese had returned to their Motherland to raise rubber on Hainan Island. And he told them about the incentives that were offered to workers on the Hainan Huaqiao Farm and how incomes increased and quality of life improved as a result. My father spoke eloquently about these things without being at all aware that his son had already decided to go and plant rubber trees.

However willing to share his recollections of pioneering Hainan's rubber production, Peng's father was anything but eager to allow his teenage son to set out on a parallel endeavor in Cultural Revolutionary Yunnan, so

I never said a word to my dad about my plans. I just took my residence permit to the local precinct.

Even though relocating from Beijing to Banna meant downward socioeco-nomic mobility, the path had to be paved with paperwork. For Beijingers of all ages, compulsory residence permits offered access to employment, ration coupons, and other urban benefits. Bureaucratic hurdles could be cleared easily enough—as Peng had discovered—by submitting a written request to surrender Beijing residency.

One Chinese institution, however, was more intractable than bureaucracy when it came to constraining individual behavior—the family. What would Father and Mother say when their teen-aged son or daughter proclaimed intentions to decamp for a distant, and possibly dangerous, frontier? Peng's reluctance to level with his family was hardly atypical. Many students kept kinfolk insulated from their project for as long as possible. Sooner or later, however, they would have to confront the issue:

> In the course of preparatory work, we did a final count of the number of Yunnan-bound *zhiqing*. There were fifty of us, the agreed-upon maximum. As our departure date drew nigh, four additional individuals including Liu Xing and Lai Weijin showed up with a petition written in their own blood, read-ing: "Struggle against selfishness, Criticize revisionism. We are determined to strengthen the frontier, transform our thought, and make ourselves a generation of revolutionary successors." They were permitted to join. Just as we were boarding the train, we also accepted a girl student named Ge Manglun who had shown up begging to join us. That made it fifty-five. After we arrived in Yunnan, three more including Li Saiyang showed up, raising our total number to fifty-eight.
>
> With the approval of the Beijing Revolutionary Committee and the Yunnan Military Council, a departure date was set: February 8, 1968.

On Chairman Mao's birthday, December 26, 1967, a ceremony was held at the Gate of Heavenly Peace:

> Tian Guang, the famous composer for the PLA's Political Department, wrote us a group song: "Surging toward the morning sun / Chairman Mao's Red Guards stride to the distant horizon." Singing the Ballad of the Labor Force, raising high our banner, we marched to Tiananmen Square to take an oath of allegiance to Chairman Mao:

If a war broke out, they would fight the American imperialists in Southeast Asia. Otherwise, they would transform Xishuangbanna within a decade. Their hearts would remain forever red, their determination steadfast.

A second, and more official send-off, for the Yunnan-bound unfolded on the afternoon of February 2 in the Beijing Eastern District Military Auditorium:

> Li Zhongqi, vice-commandant of the Beijing Defense District, which was charged with "supporting the Left" in the middle and high schools, presided and expressed the expectations and hopes that they had for us. Speeches were also given by the assistant head of the Planning Department for the Beijing City Revolutionary Committee, Liu Shuanghe, by Li Dongmin, representing the Capitol High Schools Red Guard Congress, and Wang Kuilin, representing the Yunnan Provincial Military Council's Frontier Office. Facing our family elders, our entire group of Yunnan-bound *zhiqing* stood at attention and took a solemn oath: "We hereby resolve to devote ourselves to serving the working and peasant masses and, together with the working people of the Yunnan border, carry out an arduous lifelong struggle, determined to enable Yunnan to make a still greater contribution of rubber to the Motherland."

February 8, 1968: Nothing could equal the emotional intensity of departure day. Friends, relatives, fellow students, and total strangers swarmed onto Platform 1 of the Beijing Railroad Station. For some students, such as You Hai, departure for Yunnan was a virtual declaration of independence from parental bonds:

> When the day of departure came, I told my family members not to come to see me off. But there at the station, I saw my mother and my two younger brothers in the crowd. I upbraided my mother: "Who told you to come? Don't you come crying around here!" Then I pushed them away. That is how I said goodbye to my family.
>
> But as the train whistle blew, I suddenly felt a great inner emptiness. And I spied, half lost in the crowd, the figures of my mother and brothers. She was standing there staring at the train, carrying her baby daughter. My heart was trembling. Just at that moment the whistle blew a long blast and the train lurched forward. Somebody, I don't know who, struck up our group's song: "Surging toward the Morning Sun." With tear-filled eyes, I joined in the chorus.

Peng Zhenge's recollection is less melodramatic:

> Unlike the later *zhiqing*, we didn't cry upon departure. Probably because we were a bit older—many of us around twenty-one—and because we were going with our friends.
>
> Once the train started to pull away, only a few of the girls broke down in tears. Everybody instantly started to introduce themselves around. The cadres from the Beijing Party Committee who were accompanying us also registered

their names. Some who were not previously on the list but had made their way aboard also registered.

As I recall, when we started to sign people up, there were some forty-odd. By the time we set out, there were fifty-five. Among us were a general's son, ambassadors' daughters, offspring of high-level intellectuals, kids from working class as well as capitalist and petit bourgeois families, even a few whose mothers worked as nannies, as well as children of Chiang Kai-shek's Kuomintang army officers, who were playfully called "KMT brats."

Regardless of background, we all got on famously. The oldest among us, those who had graduated from high school, were twenty-one, the youngest—a student in second-year middle—only sixteen.

Finally, recalls He Longkang, came the moment of departure:

> With a long blast of its whistle, the train carrying fifty-five youth, together with their ideals and aspirations, set out for the distant frontier.

Half a century later, planeloads of tourists board daily flights from Beijing and a few hours later descend in Jinghong to enjoy Xishuanbanna's faux Thai architecture and tropical forest theme parks. The overland journey from Beijing to the East Wind State Farm, was a ten-day ordeal though, as You Hai attests, it brought

> Fifteen minutes of fame. Accompanying the Fifty-five was their battle flag, the glory of the Premier's endorsement, and the presence of a documentary filmmaker.

In the midst of this epochal pilgrimage, a poignant vignette:

> A mother boarded the train looking for her son who had canceled his Beijing residence permit behind her back. It turned out he had boarded the train without any luggage. Like others, the boy had written in his own blood: "Struggle-Criticize-Transform Revisionism/Determined to Defend the Border/Transform Our Thinking/And Raise Up a Generation of Revolutionary Successors." Her son was still young and totally incapable of managing his own life. She begged everyone to look after him. We promised we would.
>
> What I recall best were the songs. There were half a dozen really good voices among us but as soon as someone struck up a song everyone would join in and the singing would go on for an hour or two. Besides numbers from the model dramas (*yangbanxi*), we sang the "Song of the Long March," "The East Is Red," popular Russian ballads, and other international folk songs. . . . We never regained the collective strength that came from those songs.
>
> On the train we sat by squads. . . . Every morning when we arose, we raised high our Little Red Books, faced the rising sun, and "Asked for Our Morning

Mandate" [from Chairman Mao]. At first we were unaccustomed to this, but we gradually got used to it and our slogans rang out loud and clear. The expressions on the faces of people around us ranged from confusion to astonishment. We viewed ourselves as planters, spreading the seeds of revolution.

Their way paved by Premier Zhou, the Fifty-five enjoyed first-class hospitality en route:

There were no through trains to Kunming, so we had to change at Wuhan. Arriving February 9th, we walked across the famous bridge. We stayed at the Wuchang Hotel, where we enjoyed luxurious accommodations. But because Wuchang was south of the Yangzi, we also experienced for the first time unheated rooms in the middle of the winter.

The Wuhan Revolutionary Committee sent a bus to take us to the Hankou station. We were assigned a sleeping car.

Only by traveling on the well-oiled wheels of Premier Zhou's reputation, recalls Peng Zhenge, were the Fifty-five able to cushion themselves from the chaos of Cultural Revolutionary factionalism:

In Wuhan some Rebel faction Red Guards tried to force their way onto the train. Lu Heman and I held them off. The train slowed to a halt while Beijing Revolutionary Committee officials flaunted their official letter of introduction. The train then resumed its forward progress.

Following four days of stops and starts caused by the Cultural Revolution's disruption of the rail network, the train pulled into Kunming on the morning of February 13 in the midst of a snowstorm. Newcomers had to abandon their heroic sense of mission and adjust to new realities. Their first night in Yunnan's capital was disrupted by the incessant sound of gunfire. The group, recalls You Hai, rose to the occasion:

Before the eyes of the astonished citizenry, we marched in formation through the muddy streets, flags flying, singing our songs. . . . Our stay in Kunming was just one official event after another.

Their short respite in this remote urban center forced them to modify, though not abandon, their Beijing arrogance—as Zhang Binkai remembers:

We always knew that Beijing was the best and that other places were inferior. But, no matter what, Kunming was undeniably a city. There were buses, stores with all kinds of goods, and everyone had enough to eat.

No small tribute—coming from a proud Beijinger.

On February 17, 1968, the intrepid pioneers piled into two buses and headed to Xishuangbanna.

Chapter 5

Down on the Farm

Many of Beijing's Fifty-five had viewed the film, *Beautiful Banna* depicting a tropical paradise peopled by colorful minority nationalities. A few had seen the area with their own eyes in the course of *chuanlian* or in initial exploratory trips. He Longkang had discovered an exotic panorama:

> From time to time through the mist we found ourselves looking down on a vast sea of clouds. And sometimes in this landscape of wild uninhabited mountain peaks, a minority people's hamlet would suddenly emerge in the shadow of enormous trees. Occasionally we would catch a glimpse of a woman in native dress walking past the side of our car. . . . Leaving Xiaomengyang, we found ourselves on a tortuous mountain road, twisting and turning up and down precipitous slopes . . . suddenly before us a bright panorama opened up, the famous *bazi*—a local term for valley—flowing through it like a green ribbon the Mekong River, glistening in the sunlight.

The next day on the banks of a Mekong tributary a Gauguinesque montage unfolded:

> There were people bathing in the river, the first time we had seen Dai men and women sharing a bath. The men, totally naked, used their hands to cover their private parts. The women were covered up to their breasts by sarongs, which they rolled up as they waded into the water.

While He and his friends were feasting their imaginations on this enchanting sight, local escorts regaled them with tales, merging the exotic and the erotic, of legendary Dai hospitality. But He and his confederates had not come to admire the scenery or ogle bathing beauties. They were resolved to level the triple-canopied tropical forest and replace it with productive rubber plantations. They envisioned a frontier impregnable to China's enemies (American planes were bombing just across the Vietnamese and Laotian borders). From the sweat of their brows would emerge a China proudly self-sufficient in rubber production, defying the enemy's blockade, and fiercely independent of the "Socialist Bloc" under Soviet "revisionists."

The primitive road from Kunming to Banna suffered from years of neglect. But that didn't faze the high-spirited bus riders from breaking out in song as they gawked at the majestic mountain landscape while a pair of cameramen from the Central Documentary Studio recorded the journey. At stops along the way, colorfully clad indigenous people emerged to greet the pilgrims. Fifty-fivers bested local basketball teams and, on one occasion, staged a theatrical production for indigenous inhabitants. You Hai's recollection, however, is punctuated by an ominous note. At a pit stop, Wang Kaiping pointed to a bamboo in full bloom and muttered, "This is an ill omen. There's trouble ahead." Why should this high-spirited youngster say something like this? Was he simply repeating a common myth or could he have had a premonition that Banna would become his eternal resting place?

A journey of more than three days, Peng Zhenge said,

> took us to the 5th Production Team of the Borderpoint Branch of the East Wind State Farm. So far as we could see, this was totally removed from the political struggles of the inner provinces, like an idyllic utopia. In truth, that was just our projection of our expectations.

Figure 5.1. Group picture when arriving at Da Menglong. (Chen Xinzeng collection)

For Li Man, the first impression was one of exhilaration:

> That generation of youth—we were full of ourselves. We thought we were so exalted, so great. We were going there to transform the landscape. In our

subconscious, we imagined that we were headed for a place where there was absolutely nothing. I don't know about the others, but when I got there, I discovered—my God!—the economic conditions were not all that bad. At least you had telephones, electric lights, stores. You could actually buy things. That was totally different from what I had expected. Somebody had already done some work down there.

Liu Weixiang, who had expected nothing, was pleasantly surprised:

After our arrival, we realized that our company was able to use a tractor to negotiate a stretch of road. So they already had roads! The farm welcomed us with thatched houses, a bed for every one of us and later added two tables in each house, appropriate for the young intellectuals. Each person was issued a mosquito net, a water jug that could be carried on one's back, a tin eating bowl, a stool, and bamboo storage racks for our luggage. This was much, much better than we had anticipated.

Wu Ning agreed:

We had thought conditions in Yunnan would be very rough. But it wasn't at all like that. In fact, it was much better than we had imagined. We were a newly-formed company. The houses were made of split bamboo, creating a flat surface. Roofs were thatched. Contrary to expectations, they didn't leak when it rained. Our beds were also bamboo. Everything had been prepared in advance of our arrival. Given conditions back then, everything was quite good, albeit very simple.

Others, like Yang Wansui, were disappointed but resigned:

When we first arrived, we found that there were not even brick houses for us. OK, so that's the way it was. Because we weren't familiar with local conditions, the thatched huts and rubber plantation did not live up to our expectations. But strange enough, we took it in stride and didn't see things as particularly positive or particularly negative. We just felt that's the way things are so we might as well accept them.

For Zhang Hengchi, acceptance didn't come easily:

When we got our first sight of Yunnan—good grief!—we were shocked. We immediately realized that everything we had assumed was untrue, unreal. We had been to villages around Beijing, but in those villages you could at least find newspapers, highways on which traffic could always move. In Yunnan, as soon as it rained, the highways became a sea of mud and nothing could move, nothing except oxcarts and tractors.

Grim realities of rural life gave Li Man, who had grown up in a home filled with foreign artifacts collected by her diplomat father, cause to rethink the official image of postrevolutionary China:

> Maybe because my family lived in very comfortable circumstances, when I saw the living conditions of the workers on the Farm, I was struck by the poverty. You see, I had read a lot of books, about how, after Liberation, under the leadership of the Communist Party, everybody had been enjoying a beautiful, happy life. But when I saw the real poverty of China's villages, it was not as I had imagined. So many years after Liberation, and life was still so poor.

Peng Zhenge was struck by the stark contrast between the magnificent natural environment and the grim realities of those who lived there:

> The scenery was even better than we had been told, really beautiful. The primeval tropical forest was utterly gorgeous. But life was so hard, very bitter. The production level of the Hani, the Dai—especially the Hani—had stopped at the slash-and-burn stage. When we arrived, there were no fresh vegetables—and the workload was exceedingly heavy. At that time I was small and weak and I simply couldn't take it.

Figure 5.2. Girlfriends. Fifty-fivers and members of the Dai ethnic minority. (Chen Xinzeng collection)

Figure 5.3. Group photo Squad Four. (Chen Xinzeng collection)

In any case, the Fifty-Five had not been deposited in the middle of a jungle but onto a time-honored frontier fixture—the State Farm. The East Wind Farm was modeled on borderland institutions dating to the Tang Dynasty when China's rulers had first sent armed settlers to defend the frontiers of the Middle Kingdom while cultivating the land. Established in the 1950s for precisely those purposes, the East Wind had recently become a focal point for an emerging rubber culture. Its workers included peasants and demobilized soldiers, largely from Hunan, and earlier groups of sent-down youth from cities in China's southwest. When the Fifty-five arrived, the farm was still under civilian control of Yunnan's Bureau of Agricultural Reclamation, but in the course of the Cultural Revolution, it would be taken over by the military before reverting back to civilian management. Peng Zhenge recalls life on the farm:

Reveille

Liu Xing roused us from our beds with his bugle. The soft sharp notes echoed through our thatched huts and bounced through the mountain ravines. Such a wake-up call was a real treat. At that moment, Zeng Saiwai would chime in at the top of his voice: "Dawn—has come—Sleepy pigs—get up"—which evoked peals of laughter. In fact, everyone was still half asleep.

Our Production Team Captain was Yang Chunwen, a Hani nationality army veteran, demobilized in 1958. Each morning before sunrise, Yang would muster us onto the drill field with a whistle call.

We hastily emerged from our beds, threw on our clothes, and rushed out the door. Without waiting for us to line up in formation, Captain Yang ran us up the mountain. Some of us grumbled, some tried to outrun everyone else. As soon as we got to the top of the mountain, everyone let out a yell. The sun was rising like a red ball from a sea of clouds, its rays bouncing off the mist. All we could see in the foreground were the pumpkins growing under our feet.

Captain Yang barked an order: "Everyone grab a pumpkin and see who can get it down the mountain first." And everyone galloped down the mountain with their pumpkins. . . . When some of us reached the drill field, we could still hear the voices of Huang Qiangzu and Qi Jingfan singing at the top of their lungs as they raced downhill with their pumpkins. Because they came from the heart, the songs put any music hall performance to shame.

Work

Our first job was to clear the landscape of trees, starting in the valley and working our way up. After dinner, the entire Production Team sat on the drill field surrounded by wash basins and buckets of water—fire prevention for our thatched huts. All around us the forest just cut down by the old workers was burning, flames leaping to the sky, searing the entire mountain, sparks flying upward—a soul-stirring sight.

The toughest work was digging pits for the trees on the terraced hillsides denuded by fire, under the pitiless June sun, each worker required to fill a daily quota of sixteen holes. Though nobody would criticize you if you didn't meet your quota, each of the boys worked his tail off, stripped to the waist, driven by youthful energy and a sense of pride. Hands became a mass of calluses, backs blistered from sunburn.

The girls gave their all to keep up with male comrades, You Hai recalls days toiling on the mountainside in the searing heat:

At the beginning the big problem was excessive fatigue. Wielding a hoe was utterly exhausting. You got to the point where you just couldn't move—especially by afternoon. Banna's noontime temperatures were brutal. We napped til 1:00. Then the whistle blew and everyone had to get to work. From then 'til sunset it was unbearably hot. Everybody was on the verge of fainting from heat exhaustion.

Figure 5.4. Group photo Squad Four. (Chen Xinzeng collection)

For privileged young Beijingers, every bit as onerous as the physical challenge was the ignominy of taking orders from people they viewed as social inferiors. Even after thirty years, You Hai's memories are painful:

We had all kinds of contradictions and conflicts with the Company *commanders*. That was because we had received a certain level of education; we were urbanites. Our democratic way of doing things was much stronger than theirs. The local leaders were former soldiers sent down by the army. They had been trained to treat orders from above like the Word of God. An order was an order.

Once it came down, you'd better obey without question. Moreover, they had all been brought up on the farm and then, after a stint in the army, had been sent down to serve as local leaders. Whatever they said you had to do. Anything you said fell on deaf ears. . . . We felt they were backward.

Even in the course of backbreaking work, however, You Hai found cause for joy:

During the rainy season, before setting out to work we would doff our clean clothes, give our teeth a once over lightly, change into our dirty work clothes— which were wet but cool, giving us a bracing stimulus—shoulder our hoes, and surge forward. Working up on the mountain, the wet clothes would cling to us, glued to our bodies. At this point, strains of a song would drift up through the morning's mountain mist. The singer was Chesan, an Aini worker in our production team, singing for all he was worth as he slowly passed by below us on the back of his water buffalo. Of all the minority nationality songs, none were as lovely as Chesan's. In this setting, the Aini song was like a chorus of heavenly hosts.

Leisure

Beijing youngsters somehow managed to maintain an active schedule of social activities. Former high school stars, clustered around six-foot-two center *"Da Ge"* ("Big Brother"), led the Fifty-fivers' basketball team to local championships. Others emerged with theretofore undiscovered cultural talents, most famously Peng Zhenge who won renown as virtuoso flautist and nimble dancer.

Romance

Peng Zhenge:

The first Fifty-fivers to pair off were Zhang Hengchi and Ge Manglun. When everyone else was taking an afternoon nap, they could be seen chatting with each other under the eaves in front of the girls' dorms. The sun was beating down on the empty drill field. Nobody had fallen asleep yet. There was Zhang Hengchi carrying an empty rice bowl from the girls' dorm walking across the athletic field to the boys' dorm. Through the bamboo wall I could hear Lai Weijin asking him, "What in the world were you guys talking about? Zhang said, "We were talking about *gexing jiefang*—"liberation of the individual personality"—an *au courant* expression.

Shooting the Breeze

Peng Zhenge:

> The most engaging conversationalist was Zhou Manglun. I don't know where he got hold of those military books, but he was able to discuss Soviet and American war planes, tanks, and artillery in great detail. We were a bit worried about him. If we had been in Beijing, "the walls had ears."

Malaria

Peng Zhenge:

> I was the first to come down with malaria. First a temperature of 41 degrees [105.8 degrees Fahrenheit], then shivers that rattled the bamboo bed. Fellow students ran to my side. Some wiped me off with a hot towel, some prepared medicine, some covered me with their own quilts. But nothing worked. I just lay there shivering for more than an hour while everyone stood by helpless. Zeng Silai asked me, "Pigeon, do you want something to eat? I stammered, "I—want—to—take a pee!" My voice, totally out of control, rang out loud and clear. The girls headed for the exits. Zeng got a big wash basin and I filled it. At that point I no longer shivered and fell into a deep sleep.
>
> That night my bedding was soaked through with sweat. The next morning the other students told me I had totally collapsed; they would take me to the hospital. The old workers made a bamboo stretcher and they carried me through a light rain. The road was wet, slippery, full of tractor ruts. On the way someone slipped, and I was dumped onto the road.
>
> A week later I had recovered and returned to work. People were squatting on the drill field having lunch when Zeng Silai broke everyone up with "I—want—to—pee!"

Antic humor on the military farm—however rare—was soon eclipsed by politics, as documented in Peng's memoir:

> Inevitably the ill winds of the Cultural Revolution blew into Xishuangbanna. The political factionalism of Kunming oozed its way down. At specified hours each day, morning and night, everyone had to line up in formation with a copy of "The Precious Red Book" in hand. . . . Words spoken in private were reported by other students. Farm Headquarters sent a work team to organize political study sessions and criticize "incorrect ideas." . . . I had the premonition that even though we were several thousand kilometers removed from Beijing's political whirlpool, we would sooner or later be sucked in. Together with [several] fellow high school graduates, I was sent off to the Sixth Production Team on the Qianshao Branch Farm. This place was at the foot of a pass leading over the mountains to Burma. On the other side of the border was the famous "Golden

Triangle," controlled by the Guomindang's "bandit remnants." Due to the tense security situation, the several dozen old workers on this team were all former soldiers, recently mustered out in 1965. They were Railroad Troops who had constructed the Chengdu-Kunming line through treacherous mountain terrain, with lots of tunnels—tough, dangerous work. If you take a train over that line today, you will see by the side of the tracks numerous monuments eulogizing warriors who sacrificed their lives in the line of duty. These guys told lots of sto-

Figure 5.5. Fifty-fivers at East Wind Farm 1968. All but one are from Beijing's No. 25 High School. (Chen Xinzeng collection)

ries and shared many grievances. Their bodies were scarred but they were brave guys. They had come from all over Yunnan. Some were minority nationalities, many recently married. Most of their wives were from their old hometowns. While we were working together, everyone shared jokes. We also had some "old *zhiqing*" who had been sent down from Kunming and Sichuan in the early 1960s. There were about a hundred of us in all, divided into squads.

Zhiqing as Doctor

Wang Kaiming, though not himself in the best of health, had used the Cultural Revolution to focus on the study of medicine. Having learned acupuncture and read many Barefoot Doctor books, he became the team medic. Once while I was in the mountains working in forest management, my fellow workers and I came upon a beehive overrunning with honey, which we divvied up and ate. After returning to our quarters, however, we all had belly aches. Wang Kaiming stuck a needle in my abdomen and the pain instantly disappeared.

Maoist Musings

Every evening we would hold a meeting to read *The Sayings of Chairman Mao* or recite the "Three Basic Essays." In private we groused about this kind of formalistic study. One of the retired soldiers said he had been illiterate and had never gone to school but had conquered his illiteracy by reading *The Sayings of Chairman Mao.*

At one point the Rebel mob surrounded us and prepared to subject all of us to the Drowning Dog treatment [throwing the victim into a pond]. In the nick of time several dozen students came and dragged us off.

Home Leaves

According to regulations, military farm *zhiqing* were entitled to periodic home leaves. Even during the worst of times, prospect of a family reunion gave exiled Beijingers cause for hope. But during the turbulent Cultural Revolution, leaves frequently took youngsters to remote places to which evicted family members had been relocated—political punishment thinly disguised under rubrics such as "revolutionary education." Valuable time was taken up traveling over vast distances.

On one home leave, Peng Zhenge had to tend to the sad task of seeing his father off to a May 7th Cadre School—a Cultural Revolutionary institution designed to take vengeance on designated class enemies. Accompanied by Lin Ni, Peng undertook the three-and-a-half-day bus trip to Kunming followed by three days by rail to Beijing. For the first half of the train journey, they stood in the aisle—until they were fortunate enough to secure berths. Upon arrival in Beijing, Peng discovered that the five members of his household had been scattered across the map of China.

Yunnan's Factional Warfare Turns Violent

Quite soon the political climate on the farm heated up and pressures on us increased. At meetings large and small, whenever the leaders spoke, they would criticize us—without mentioning names—for our "inadequate awareness of the political line." The family of our Li Xiansu were close friends with Tan Furen, who was Yunnan's kingpin—chair of the Provincial Revolutionary Committee and a member of the political committee of the Kunming Military District. So, whenever she went home on leave, she always stayed with the Tan family in Kunming and gave him a report. She told them about what was going on at the grassroots level—the lineups to draw political demarcations, the armed struggle.

On December 17, 1970, Tan Furen and his wife were murdered in their home.

Chapter 6

A Reign of Terror

Just when we were giving everything we had, we were labeled "a pile of petty bourgeois intellectuals," "capitalist restorationists," and were tossed to the four winds. . . . Even now we find this hard to believe.

—You Hai

Beginning in the late 1960s, internecine struggles tore apart the fabric of Chinese society—in every government and Party bureau, factory, and school. Though conflicts were inseparable from Beijing-based Cultural Revolutionary politics, each was shaped by local factors. The East Wind Farm was no exception.

There were two major political cliques in Yunnan—the 8–23 or "Eights" Faction and the Bombardier Faction. The Bombardiers took their name from Mao's famous big character poster, "Bombard the Headquarters." The Eights took theirs from the twenty-third day of the eighth month—August 23, 1968—when Kunming Red Guards had assaulted city and provincial Communist Party headquarters. Though factional constellations varied from place to place, the Bombardiers had ties with the Party establishment dating from the CCP underground organization of the late 1940s. The Eights were connected to the military.

By February 1968, when the Beijing Fifty-five arrived on the scene, factional rivalry had escalated into armed combat in the streets of Kunming. On the East Wind Farm, however, the situation was relatively stable until the middle of the year, when the farm's Communist Party became so deeply entangled in factional conflict that it no longer was able to function. At that point, the Farm was placed under military control. The key figure was Song Tianming, a military officer determined to wrest Farm management from established leaders and to consolidate power under the Eights. Li Saiyang recalls:

In August 1968, we were all enlisted in the East Wind Farm's Jiafeng Branch, Company Five. Because the State Farm's Party Committee was paralyzed and inoperative, we had been placed under military control. The Chair of the Military Committee was Song Tianming (at the time he was Assistant Chief of Staff for the Simao Military District).

In 1969, determined to consolidate power in his own hands, Song Tianming, in league with a confederate named Li, took it upon himself to initiate a movement to "Draw a Line of Demarcation in the Lineup." Any cadres and ordinary folk who were considered to have joined the wrong side were cruelly criticized and struggled against.

Ruthless and vindictive, Song put into play the unyielding determination that had won him medals on the battlefield. Prime targets of his recruitment efforts were the Beijing Fifty-five. If Song could mobilize the intellectual resources, ideological dedication, and youthful energy of this group, his crusade to win control of the Farm would come that much closer to realization.

Flattered to be courted, some Fifty-fivers were more than ready to ingratiate themselves with an individual able to grant access to entry-level positions in the hierarchy of Farm leadership. They were happy to work with Song or, at very least, to avoid challenging him. A greater number, however, hesitated to become entangled in the kind of factional intrigue that had alienated them from Red Guard politics in their native Beijing. These loosely affiliated alliances became labeled, respectively, "Minority Faction" and "Majority Faction." A prominent figure among the Minority was He Longkang. Having initiated the Yunnan venture, He took more of a personal interest in politics on the farm than did most of his cohorts. Leaders of the Majority Faction included Su Baikai, Lin Ni, and Wang Zhenzha. You Hai, though sharply critical of the Minority, now sees both factions with a critical eye:

People such as He Longkang and Li Xi believed that we in the majority faction looked down upon the workers. What did they mean by that? They meant that we were here to be educated. . . . That was something we all had to accept. The likes of Li Xi felt that's simply the way it was. Some of our fellow students were quite arrogant . . . thought that they were better than other people. Our majority faction included some people like that, just as Americans look down on American Indians. When we went down to the local level, we found the folks were very poor, so we thought we could help them, educate them—not be educated *by* them—and that there was no way we could base our lives and customs on theirs, no way we could adopt those backward characteristics.

So, after we arrived, we were always bent on asserting ourselves. We felt we could accomplish something, whether our motives were positive or negative. This is how the split between our two factions began. He Longkang and those people began to feel that our faction was arrogant, always picking fault with one leader or another, always believing that we were in the right. If we behaved like that, how in the world were we going to get educated?

From the beginning people like He Longkang and Liang Bangmei also wanted to make a name for themselves, to elevate themselves. But their way of thinking about those on top was different from ours. They cozied up to the local powers and conveyed the message that "we really like you; we really respect you." In fact, they didn't necessarily feel that way. They were just trying to get ahead. But some such as Su Baikai and Lin Ni were also trying to promote themselves, though they went about it in a different way. Then there were people like Wu Sibing who acted deviously, very deceitfully. They pretended to accept reeducation from the poor and lower-middle peasants, pretended to obey them but the reality was a completely different thing. They were just trying to cozy up to show that they were the ones who most readily accepted education at the hands of the poor and lower-middle peasants. In reality they were less receptive to this discipline than anyone else, the least prepared to endure hardships, and the most unscrupulously ambitious.

Policy matters, says You Hai, also came into play:

> After the state farms were established, there was an emphasis on rubber produc-
> tion, no matter what the consequences for basics of livelihood—food, housing,
> and clothing. . . . But then there was a Movement to Study Dazhai, which meant
> to be agriculturally self-sufficient. So they turned around and planted grain.
> First they'd say it was OK to raise pigs, then it was not OK. . . . We went down
> there to plant rubber trees to defeat American imperialism. So far as we were
> concerned, we should be planting rubber trees, not wavering back and forth.

Underlying particular issues were the unpredictable political oscillations of the Cultural Revolution and bureaucratic imperatives of Party and State that guided policies at every level. Though driven by ideals of self-sacrifice in a higher cause, the Beijing Fifty-five found it dangerous to take the initiative. Assigned to raising vegetables, Little Li became the target of official wrath when she distributed seedlings to units other than her own. "What we're look- ing at here," reflected You Hai, "is simply bureaucratism."

Failing to win over the greater number of the Beijing Fifty-five, Song Tianming came to view these intractable youngsters as a viper in his bosom. So long as educated urbanites continued to live and work together in the high-profile Company Five of the Jiangfeng Branch Farm, they would be positioned to mobilize opposition to his authority. The solution was to break them up and send them individually or in small groups to serve in the Farm's far-flung work units. The expression was to "*chan shazi*"—"to mix the grains of sand."

Even after four decades, poignant memories of departure day continued to haunt Peng Zhenge:

As we were being loaded onto tractors, nobody said a word. Wang Guangfeng, Li Chengan, and the other old workers loaded basket after basket of papayas, sugar cane, and pineapples onto our carts. The tractors started up and everyone burst into tears. I felt a tightness in my throat, and suddenly I started to cry. But I felt that I wasn't really crying. I was really roaring, howling like a wolf.

Wherever they relocated, however, Beijingers remained under the thumb of Song Tianming. Peng Zhenge was one of four transferred to Production Team 6 at the Qianshao Branch Farm:

On one occasion Farm Headquarters held a Struggle Meeting. Each work team placed dunce caps on the heads of members designated as "Bombardier Faction," "capitalist roaders" or "Five Black Elements," hung signs around their necks, and gave each an old wash basin to beat. We then formed a column and followed our leaders to Farm Headquarters in Damenglong, shouting slogans as we marched. That was a Sunday, a market day, so there were lots of Dai women on the street, dressed in colorful sarongs, hair festooned with orchids, carrying their baskets through the street market. When they saw our column, they ran off laughing.

At the Menglong Bridge, we spied a young man bathing in the river below. When he saw our column, he stood there staring at us, legs squeezed together, naked as a jaybird. I laughed to myself and wished I had a camera to capture the scene. This would have been my photo: In the foreground this naked boy. In the middle, this ridiculous line of marchers, on the side of the bridge, a line of Dai girls relieving themselves, like a flock of ducklings, also facing the bridge and looking at us, and in the background the beautiful blue sky, white clouds, dark mountains, and green water. . . .

But my memory must be playing tricks. This was a cloudy, cold winter day. As our column of marchers reached Menglong Street, several dozen columns from different Work Teams had already gathered. The first one to have arrived had begun its "Beating the Drowning Dog" ritual. This involved pulling out the team member who was under attack, lifting him up by his four limbs and, 1—2—3, heaving him into the fishpond. A cacophony of noise and slogans erupted and from the pond emerged a soaking wet figure clad in black.

The Rebels on the bank taunted him to crawl back up, only to throw him in again. The whole area was in an uproar. I stood on the outside of the crowd, suppressing a laugh until I realized that the pond was festooned with punji sticks to deter people from stealing fish, and some people had clearly been wounded. My heart skipped a beat. I couldn't bear to keep looking. As I turned to leave, I saw the Fifth Work Team from the Jiangfeng farm approach. The victim at the head of the column was the "capitalist roader" Yang Chunwen, a retired soldier who was our old Team captain. We Fifty-five had worked under him for a whole year after arriving from Beijing.

The leaders of the "Rebel" faction had to abide by their factional principles and carry out violent struggle. We students had made a few suggestions, for which our reward was to be scattered among other Work Teams. In the process, Yang Chunwen had been pulled into the struggle for serving as our pillar of support. When I saw Old Yang, who had always walked proud and tall, reduced to this state, my blood boiled.

At the epicenter of this melodrama, recalls Li Saiyang, Song Tianming was a foreboding presence:

They even tried to drag out Yang Chunwen, the captain of Team Five who had worked side by side with us day and night, and throw him too into the fish-pond. But we old Beijing *zhiqing* surrounded them while Liu Anyang shouted, "Struggle with words, not weapons!" Wang Kaiping stepped forward and shielded Yang Chunwen with his own body.

At this moment, Song Tianming—in mufti—charged forward, working the crowd and stirring up support, shouting "They are all Liandong elements" [referring to a vilified faction of Beijing Red Guards]. The resistance on the part of the old Beijing *zhiqing* enraged Song Tianming. That very same day they detained every one of the Fifty-fivers on the scene for a "study session" at Farm Headquarters. Anyone who objected to what they were doing would not be allowed to return to his or her work team.

During a "study session" that lasted until dawn, . . . Song Tianming proclaimed that he represented the armed struggle faction. The contest between them and us—the cadres and masses who had lined up on the wrong side—was one of life and death. They would fight us just like the old days when we fought the Japanese demons and the Guomindang army. It would be utterly merciless. . . .

"Even if you came down here with the backing of Premier Zhou, we still wonder which side you are really on. You need to be re-educated. If you persist in your errors, the revolutionary masses will not fall for your tricks. If you don't think I'm serious, just try me. Do what you will. I'll have the last word! If I weren't here today, you would all be drowning dogs."

He spoke with panache, put on a real show. He boasted of how he had played the good cop/bad cop game to expose countless capitalist roaders, Five Black Elements, class enemies, anti-military, and insubordinate military elements on the East Wind Farm. He said he would run every one of them to the ground and would never let them get back up.

Fifty-fivers, recalls Peng Zhenge, did not take this challenge lying down:

Su Baikai, Lin Ni, Zeng Silai, and others declared that "Beating the Drowning Dog" was in direct violation of the Center's policy of "Struggle with civil means, not military means."

But Song was not about to brook criticism from a bunch of young whippersnappers still wet behind the ears. His vengeance, says Li Saiyang, was relentless:

> From this point on the entire East Wind State Farm was shrouded in a miasma of terror. One after another, word came of people struggled to death or taking their own lives. At the time I was serving as Vice-Chair of the Revolutionary Committee of the Farm's Team Three. This was precisely the cradle of the revolution, the fountainhead for the "319" rebels. We witnessed level upon level (State Farm, Branch Farm, Production Team), time after time (each accused person had to go through the ordeal on at least three separate occasions), and utterly inhuman criticism-struggle sessions. We saw Song Tianming strutting around baring his fangs and claws, even to the point of threatening people with a gun. At the same time, we could see him lecherously ogling our girl students, frequently sending his military motor pedicab to the work teams to bring back female students for "discussion" or "study." One of these girls returned from a meeting with him totally out of her senses. We have heard nothing of her since. Wu Shutao, an old worker with whom I had very good relations, was dragged out to discuss a "problem" and ended up, on a stormy windy night, hanging himself in the middle of the rubber plantation.

Political Struggle Intensifies

> After "Beating the Drowning Dog," physical assaults against political targets became more and more severe. Some "objects of struggle" were thrown into the cesspool. On Sundays my fellow students and I would often walk more than ten kilometers to get together and talk about what was going on. We even discussed the possibility of taking our case to the provincial authorities.

Even after the "scattering of the grains of sand," the struggle continued in different forms in far-flung milieus. Peng Zhenge:

> Zeng Silai was the leader among the four of us. . . . He had a natural sense of humor and was full of tricks. He was short of stature, with big round eyes and a broad mouth that was always smiling. He looked mischievous but he was really kind-hearted and sympathetic. Zeng's father was a PLA general from Jiangxi. Zeng had lived his entire life on army bases. When the Cultural Revolution broke out, his father feared he would be led astray so he sent him to an army camp in Inner Mongolia to experience several months of military life. Thus, he immediately hit it off with our Team's army veterans. He was not above sharing risqué jokes with them.

Fifty-fivers' grassroots camaraderie with army veterans by no means deterred Song Tianming from continuing his vendetta:

From this point on, no matter which Production Team we were in, all of us were designated by the leadership as targets to be subjected to criticism under the rubric that our "understanding of the political line" was "inadequate."

Because they were stationed close to the volatile Burmese border, Peng and fellow Beijingers were issued firearms, albeit, without ammunition. Though weapons rusted into uselessness in the tropical humidity, being designated part of the nation's frontier defense force provided a much-needed fillip to self-esteem. Not for long:

One day our Team Captain, took away my gun, saying it was upon orders from above. I was very upset. So I wrote a letter to the vice-chair of the Farm Revolutionary Committee, Li Xiuqi. I said I had come to the borderland to contribute to economic construction and border defense. Therefore, I took offense at having my gun taken away. Later, at a meeting of the whole branch farm, Li Xiuqi said, "Some people have expressed resentment at having their guns confiscated. With people like you, lacking in political consciousness, there is a real question at whom you might aim your weapons." This upset me even more. The pressure was becoming intense. From then on, there were no more mock combat exercises for our team and little intermixing between the old workers and us.

Most of Song's vengeance, writes Peng Zhenge, fell on defenseless subordinates in the Farm organization, individuals that the young Beijingers were powerless to protect:

They couldn't drag out any "counter-revolutionaries" from our Qianshao Sixth Team. After all, everybody was a retired soldier. But the order from above was that every team, no matter what, had to expose people from the "Five Black Classes" and the Cannon Faction. So they dragged out a retired soldier named Geng.

Old Geng was a man of few words. But, complaining about this or that, he may have once uttered a few indiscrete comments. In any case, they labeled him as having a "counter-revolutionary history."

On one occasion, our Team was having a Criticism Meeting and the Team Captain ordered me and the other young men to attend. They said that today we would criticize the "counter-revolutionary history" guy, Old Geng. Then, they said, we'd subject him to a "Beat the Drowning Dog" session in the fishpond.

I had always been very much opposed to military struggle. But under the circumstances, I didn't know if I wanted to expose myself or if it would be wiser to avoid trouble, given the fact that I had clashed with the Rebel faction on prior occasions. I thought, well, we'll do whatever the Captain tells us to do. Anyway, Old Geng was charged with having a "counter-revolutionary history," which had nothing to do with factional struggle.

The meeting was reaching its climax and the Captain was standing on the podium waving his hand and ordering, "Drag Geng up here." So, together with another student and several old workers, I pushed him forward. Old Geng was also totally submissive. From the podium and from the audience came the shouts, "Give Geng the Drowning Dog treatment." As we were dragging him to the fishpond, he said to us, "Take it easy, OK?" We nodded our heads and threw him in legs first. There was a great splash. Then Old Geng emerged and stood up. I could see his soaking wet body festooned with strands of water plants. I felt totally beside myself. Taking it all in stride, Old Geng crawled up and, dripping wet, followed the crowd, everybody shouting slogans, back to the meeting hall.

I carry my guilt feeling toward Old Geng right up to the present day. From that experience, I took away a warning: Never again allow myself to play the role of a henchman in a political movement.

Malarial Mayhem

After the June rainy season had passed, we returned to the mountains to plant rubber trees, working at a high level of intensity. One noon, I came down with another attack of malaria, running a fever of forty-one to forty-two degrees centigrade. Once you have contracted malaria, it keeps coming back year after year.

As I was lying on my cot, bathed in my own sweat, my brother ran up the mountain and asked leave from the Team Captain to take me to the infirmary. When the Captain refused, he rushed back and, after getting off work, got Wang Peimin to give me an injection and some medication to lower my fever.

That evening, I wrapped myself in a quilt and went to the meeting, held on the basketball court in the middle of our compound. The only light we had came from a few dim lamps in the surrounding buildings. People were sitting all over the place. The Team Captain, as was his custom at these evening meetings, stood by a lamp to deliver his pep talk. In his usual mawkish manner, he rambled on about everything under the sun, from production to politics. Finally, he changed his tone. Without mentioning names, he said that the Beijing students suffered from low political awareness. They needed thought reform. The more I heard, the madder I got. When he finally finished, I wrapped my quilt around my shoulders, stood up, and walked to the lamp by the loudspeaker. I said, "Let me add a few words." At this point, retired soldiers, old housewives, *zhiqing*, everyone, with a whoosh, grabbed their stools, crowded around me, and listened intently.

"Who said we have a low level?" I asked. Do they even have to confiscate my gun? Do they have to keep me from going to the infirmary when I come down with malaria? . . . " When I finished talking, I returned to my place and sat down. The Captain was furious. Ranting incoherently, he said: "What's gotten into you all? When I talk, you sit every which way all around the court but when Peng Zhenge talks, you draw in close. This is too much! . . . "

With the meeting effectively adjourned, in the dim light among the people turning to go home I thought I could spot a few struggling to conceal their grins.

That night Wang Huimin gave me some medication. The next morning I got up late. Not until I was outside brushing my teeth did I see the Captain squatting in a corner across from our barracks. Several wives of retired soldiers were gathered nearby gesturing in his direction and laughing at him. It was said that his wife hadn't allowed him to enter his own house.

For the Fifty-five, isolated and powerless on a remote frontier, opportunities to savor revenge against imperious officials did not come often.

Whatever doubts local leaders might have had about the political reliability of the Fifty-five did not deter them from using these youngsters in drives to recruit more urban youth for service on the frontier. While Peng Zhenge was on home leave in Beijing, he agreed to give a talk to students at his alma mater, No. 25 High School. When Peng found an official recruiter from his Farm sharing the podium, he realized that an unvarnished account of frontier rigors would bring repercussions when he returned to Yunnan, so

I talked about life in the Jiangfeng Team Five. I talked about how students labored together, how good the old workers were toward us. I didn't forget to describe Xishuangbanna's natural environment, the kind of grasses that scratched, the kind of insects that bit. I painted a rich picture of life in Xishuangbanna. What I didn't discuss was the factional struggle. Later the official who had come to Beijing to recruit said that my talk had persuaded a great many people to go down to Xishuangbanna.

A Death in the Family

Mixing guts and guile, fortitude and resignation, Peng and the others managed to endure lives of hard work and devastating disease, backbreaking labor, and persecution. Though scattered around the countryside, they retained personal ties and feelings of group identity. Early in 1970 they reassembled—for a funeral.

Here is Peng Zhenge's account:

Ling Yu was my fellow student, the same year but different homerooms. His parents were rightists. In 1958 they had been sentenced to reform through labor. Relying on his older sister, he was able to complete high school. Ling Yu was an introvert, a man of few words who seldom smiled. But he was kind and straightforward. Physically strong, he put everything he had into his work. As I remember him, he was always bare-chested, wielding a hoe. From time to time we would see him in the mountains, his back baked brown by the sun. In the evening he would be sitting on his bed reading under the mosquito net. He reminded me of Jean Valjean in Hugo's *Les Misérables*. In the political movements of the era, he was, like the rest of us. He didn't opportunistically identify with the Rebel faction. He just threw himself into his work, silently but with even greater dedication.

In 1969 Ling Yu volunteered to join a newly established production team in a remote area. Every day, according to what I heard, he was the very last to come down the mountain—and he insisted on carrying down a tree trunk to use as construction material for their housing. When he arrived, the rice was already cold, so he just heated it up with a bit of boiling water and ate. He was always going around quietly helping those who needed it.

March 15, 1970, was a night of thunderstorms. I walked more than 10 *li* [5 kilometers] from the headquarters of the branch farm to the place where his work team was laboring. I found him in his room spitting up blood and a kind of green bile. His condition had obviously reached a critical state. His classmate Wang Huimin, who was serving as team medic, gave him some medicine, and it appeared that his condition had stabilized somewhat. Together with some of his team's old workers, we wanted to take him to the infirmary, but he adamantly refused to go.

The next morning the rain stopped. Ling Yu was already deliriously ill. So Wang Huimin and I, together with some old workers, carried him to the infirmary of the 5th Branch Farm. As soon as the doctor saw his condition, he had an ambulance take him to the State Farm hospital.

Two days later Ling Yu died of amoebic dysentery. That day nearly all Beijing Fifty-five gathered at the headquarters of the Qianshao Branch Farm. We stood around Ling Yu's body. The old workers placed him in a black wooden coffin. The girls sat around him, strewing him with white flowers. I don't have a clear recollection of how we passed that night. Early the next morning nearly everybody on the farm—male, female, old, and young—came for a memorial service. The boys vied for the honor of carrying his coffin. Then we walked to the burial site. The grave was on a small mountain where the Number Three Work Team was located. As we walked up the mountain, some of my fellow students came to relieve me in carrying the coffin. I looked back to see about a thousand people in the funeral procession, including old workers, old women, all of them wiping tears from their eyes.

By the time we had buried Ling Yu and held the ceremony, it was noon, and everybody went their own way. But Song Tianming summoned the Beijing students together. He said a few things, of which I recall only one: "Nobody should talk any more about what happened in the past. If anyone does, they will be held responsible."

The grief-stricken students could only listen in numbed silence. Looking back upon these events, however, Peng Zhenge gave voice to a consensus that they had been victims of history:

After thirty years, all I can do, in my simple way, is write about what happened in the past. And I don't see that there's anything for which I should be held responsible.

In retrospect, most Fifty-fivers would agree that the immediate cause of Ling Yu's death was amoebic dysentery but that politics had rendered him vulnerable to the ravages of disease. In his determination to overcome an unfavorable class background through revolutionary self-sacrifice, Ling Yu had worked himself to death.

At the time, however, at least some of the Fifty-five saw their comrade's premature demise through the lens of revolutionary orthodoxy. You Hai's diary entry for March 17, 1970:

"Whenever there is struggle, there is bound to be sacrifice."—Mao Zedong

Today at 9:45 a.m. one of our 55, Ling Yu died. I took an oath to Chairman Mao. Facing Ling Yu's photo, I swore:

"On the great road of uniting with the workers and peasants, I will follow the teachings of Chairman Mao: 'One don't fear hardship, two don't fear death.' . . . As long as I live, I will do my utmost, I will happily shed my warm blood for the people, I will be prepared to go to war at any moment, and will never rest until we have turned the entire world Red."

Chapter 7

Life and Labor Post-Diaspora

Thrown into an alien environment, the Beijing Fifty-fivers struggled to negotiate meaningful, productive lives. Alternatives to grueling labor under the tropical sun were hard to come by. Compounding the dilemma was the bitter truth that they had volunteered to carve rubber plantations out of a wilderness. Logically speaking, they had chosen this life of labor. By virtue of family background and educational status, however, they were potentially more useful in other roles—if only their skills could be appreciated and utilized by the local leadership.

Poignant details about the diaspora lives of the Beijing Fifty-five emerge from the testimony of You Hai. Eager to prove her worth, You had volunteered for wilderness duty. She was assigned to head up a group of ten *zhiqing*, all males. You and her comrades worked in competitive tandem with another squad led by her boyfriend, Yin Zheng—already legendary for his feats of physical prowess and superhuman endurance.

Plunging into the tangled jungle growth, the young pioneers begged hospitality from Hani villagers, sleeping around an open fireplace in the middle of a hut. Shouldering machetes, they marched forth each morning to carve primitive passageways through the underbrush. They slept in makeshift roadside tents fashioned from tree branches and sheets of plastic, subsisting on a monthly ration of forty pounds of state-subsidized rice.

Team members slashed their way upward into the hills, following mountain streams until they found land level enough to grow vegetables for self-sustenance. Makeshift mattresses were woven from trees felled and grass cut in their wilderness clearing campaign. The thorny grass so lacerated You's hands that, by day's end, she was barely able to open her fist. Relief came after sunset, when she returned to the base camp at the foot of the mountains, where boiled water provided by the kitchen crew enabled her to unclench her pustule-covered hands.

Though romantically linked comrades in arms, Yin and You were die-hard rivals. The intrepid Yin would scramble up treacherous slope to stake out

Figure 7.1. Fifty-fivers at Fengguang sub-farm. East Wind Farm 1969. Yin Zheng is the third from left. (You Heng collection)

Figure 7.2. Digging terraces with hoes. (Chen Xinzeng collection)

Figure 7.3. Building a bridge. (Chen Xinzeng Collection)

land for his squad, leaving You and her entourage with whatever was left over. Yin would also mark "his" trees—valuable resources for construction and cooking. If anyone else cut down a tree in his area, he would fell another to pin it to the ground, rendering it inaccessible to competitors. So bitter was inter-squad hostility that some resorted to flattening the tires of rivals' pushcarts.

Competition notwithstanding, as volunteers driven by revolutionary élan and personal pride, the Fifty-five could be capable of extraordinary feats of sacrifice and endurance:

Sometimes we staged contests to see how many hours of work we could do in a day. We would set out at 7 in the morning and work up on the mountain until noon. After an hour's break for lunch, we would work again until 5. Some of our *gung-ho* guys added a night shift facilitated by the light of little oil lamps. Our big competitions were called "campaigns." We had large campaigns and small campaigns, the former involving 12-to-16-hour days. If I put in fewer hours than the others, they would call me "arrogant."

FROM WORKER TO PROPAGANDIST

Over the course of time, squads like You's and Yin's built frontier settlements where more workers could join forces for large-scale deforestation, terracing, and planting of rubber trees.

The Fifty-five were also valuable assets for jobs requiring education, leadership skills, and specialized talents. Such assignments provided at least temporary relief from the grueling labor. Opportunities to move upward and outward, however, came, at the very least, with implicit conditions. Accepting a leader's offer of a desirable job invariably brought entanglements—personal, political, and ideological. This was especially true for members of the propaganda corps. With its focus on communication, propaganda was an ideal arena for the Fifty-fivers to strut their stuff. Because they spoke standard northern mandarin, young Beijingers were uniquely qualified to perform in revolutionary dramas. After months of backbreaking labor, such an opportunity to draw upon their urban legacy was hard to pass up. However, it was challenging, to say the least, for Fifty-fivers to make propaganda on behalf of people whose politics, ideology, and values were so foreign to their own. You Hai—who had already done an initial tour of duty in the propaganda corps—was now asked to do another. Her diary entry is terse:

> I found myself involved in an intense personal ideological struggle. I simply couldn't do it.

She recalled that

> Song Tianming and those people were the Rebel Faction. They sent me to work in the propaganda corps so that I could disseminate their revolutionary line or whatever. At that time, I was very much opposed to them. I had reached the conclusion that they were acting incorrectly, so I didn't want to join their corps, didn't want to perform for them or write scripts—I simply didn't want to go. The first time I went to the propaganda corps the contradictions between us were not so clear or so sharp. This time they would want us to propagandize the Rebel Faction's songs, etc. They were members of the 3.19 faction so there would invariably be one or two programs that propagandized their line. Furthermore, they wanted me to go as a single individual. I felt I couldn't do anything on that basis.
>
> Even though unwilling, I finally went because in the last analysis you had to do what the leader told you to do.

YIN-THE-INDESTRUCTIBLE

As You Hai struggled to prove herself in an alien environment, Yin Zheng served as a living reminder of her own illusions. Next to him, she was painfully aware not only of how far she fell short of revolutionary ideals but of the pitiful inadequacy of her concept of self and her mission in life. Yin was both an inspiration and a reproach:

> When I was trying to get into a university but had not yet succeeded, Yin sent me a letter. He talked about many heroes and teachings of Mao, such as China ought to make a great contribution to mankind. The whole thing was full of heroic figures of speech . . . I felt I wanted to throw myself into the revolution, as a dedicated leftist.
>
> Yin Zheng was different. Later, in a conversation with me, he said that I had allowed myself to "board the bandit boat." I said, "What's that all about? I went to the countryside to throw myself into the revolution. How can you say I 'boarded the bandit boat'"? He wasn't like me. He came to the frontier with a coldly calculating attitude. He said, "I'm not like you guys, running down here in the heat of passion." He was extremely cool-headed.
>
> Yin had no choice but to come down since his mother had contracted uterine cancer and had to be operated on and his father was shut up in a "cowshed" [detention facility].
>
> He said: "I am a man of cold reason. I'm not like you who come here to turn the world upside down." I had made the mistake of "boarding the bandit boat." He said that when this gang [the Fifty-five] came down, they were all driven by ambition. But actually he had come with no ambitions whatever, none of that heroic posturing.

Half a century later, thanks to current ecological knowledge and sensitivity, the destruction of Banna's triple-canopy tropical rain forest and its replacement by shallow-rooted rubber trees has brought about second thoughts about the "patriotic mission" to turn Yunnan's southwest frontier into China's number two source of latex. At the time, few were troubled by environmental issues, least of all the Beijing Fifty-five. A singular exception was Yin Zheng, who

> felt that from the beginning, wholesale destruction of forests to plant rubber trees was not right. At that time Yin Zheng wrote a lot of things. He said that leveling the primeval forest would have an impact on the climate and for that reason rubber production was unsustainable. He wrote an article with this analysis.

Yin, however, was no crusader for environmentalism—or, for that matter, any other ism. He was, recalls You, "very unorthodox but not a rebel":

He just thought more deeply than the rest of us. But he wasn't one to speak out. He just did his work. So he was admired as a model by the cadres as well as by the other *zhiqing*.

"Somewhere," You recalls,

I have a photo of Yin Zheng cutting down a huge tree, a banyan tree so big that several people could not get their arms around it. It took him a week to cut it down. By the time the tree fell, the ax cuts were higher than the height of a man. Yin's hands were covered with blisters. He was like an ascetic monk. . . .

Yin Zeng drank urine, you know. He drank urine while he was up on the mountain where the two of us had gone to cut grass. There was no water, so the work was terribly tough. It was brutally hot. We climbed to the summit. Who was going to send up water to you? Finally, we were too thirsty to take it—so Yin Zheng drank urine. He told us after we had come down. His throat was burning dry, and his hands ached, and there was the scorching sun.

What made Yin Zheng unique was his ability to throw himself, body and soul, into a mission he deemed quixotic and to follow through without a hint of cynicism or hypocrisy. Recommended for Battalion Commander, Yin quickly became a Party member. Not surprisingly, after completing his tour in the countryside and enlisting in the Chinese Air Force, he quickly rose through the ranks. He had little time to bask in the limelight. In 2006, at age fifty-seven, he suffered a fatal heart attack. Yin-the-Indestructible had burned himself out.

Even Stakhonovites such as Yin Zheng found time for leisure activities. As You Hai recalls, the Fifty-five read whatever they could, whenever they could:

I had no personal property back then, only books. . . . When I left China, I had two or three thousand volumes. . . . I'd buy anything. Stories of heroes, the collected speeches of Castro. There wasn't much getting published during the Cultural Revolution so I'd buy whatever I could get my hands on.

Going to the movies meant seeing the "Eight Model Plays." It meant walking two hours to get there. We saw some of them two or three, even seven or eight, times. Why? Because that was all there was. A person would sit there watching it and could sing along from beginning to end. This was a way of filling an empty space in our lives. There simply wasn't anything else. . . . For example, I would come there from the East Wind Farm and he from Qianxiao. We'd talk, get to see each other. It was a chance to get together.

After the film, we would sleepwalk our way back. It was so late, and we had been working hard all day. I remember us, everybody holding hands, walking back, a journey of an hour or two. I would keep my eyes open and pull you along while you slept. There was no other way, nothing was really good, but we had to go, that's just the way our life was. Later we joined hands because we were afraid of wandering off and getting lost. The two on the inside would sleep, those on the outside would walk, then we'd switch off. . . .

We had flashlights but I used mine as little as possible—because I was a revolutionary, so everyone would say I wasn't arrogant.

POLITICAL LIFE

By recruiting You Hai for propaganda work, Party leaders had recognized her as a person of political reliability, indeed a candidate for Party membership. For a young Chinese, admission to the CCP was a major step up the ladder of success. You Hai was asked to apply early in the diaspora when she was transferred to Mengla, but deemed herself unworthy. "I felt the Party was so sacred," she recalled:

They wanted to admit me, but I felt I wasn't sufficiently qualified. Actually, at that time I wanted to enter the Party—and I eventually did. . . . I was always very modest. . . . I never sought to draw attention to myself. I always thought I was not up to it. So I did not consent.

Finally admitted to China's elite club,

they made me Assistant Regimental Party Secretary. The guy in the Battalion Party branch (he's dead now) liked me a lot. His name was Wei Zhiyi. He was a rough and tumble cadre, a worker-peasant cadre, but he had a heart. He made a lot of mistakes, but he was a good man. Those guys couldn't write. Later they gave me the responsibility of writing the Party committee reports. But I used to say to them, I labor in the Company ranks all day and come here to write at night. So (from then on) I went there every morning, to Battalion headquarters, to write for them.

Party membership, as You soon realized, made it impossible to avoid factional entanglements. "We are really conflicted about class struggle," she confessed in her diary. Interviewed years later, she explained:

I was good friends with Yang Tiangui, an old cadre who had just joined our Company. Yin Zheng was also his good friend. He was sent to our Company for discipline because he was a capitalist roader. He had been the top leader of the East Wind Farm—a really big cadre. He was "sent down" to work with us, a way of criticizing him and beating him down. He carried buckets of shit every day. This guy was interesting. Later everyone said he used such stratagems to establish ties with the younger generation. I was indifferent to all this. At that time the guy who wanted to beat him down and criticize him was Li Xiuqi.

Li Xiuqi was later at the State Farm Headquarters. He was a Hunanese, a member of the Rebel Faction, on very good terms with He Longkang and those guys. There were two types of them: One was the retired cadres, the other was the Hunanese. I don't know if he's still alive. This guy was really thoughtful. He understood us very well. Actually he was extremely leftist.

You Hai's struggle to negotiate a path between Yang and Li illustrates how politically ambitious *zhiqing* carved their way through the tangled political landscape. They tried their best to maintain self-respect, to be true to their comrades, to their revolutionary commitments, to themselves. But opportunities did not come knocking every day. When they did, one had to be quick to respond. Among other things, *zhiqing* learned to overlook ideological and factional differences and to appreciate admirable human qualities wherever they found them.

The faith of true believers might inspire youthful innocents in Beijing, but ideological absolutes had negative survival value in the challenging landscape of frontier politics.

Chapter 8

The Fifty-five in Flood Tide

On December 22, 1968—ten months after the Fifty-fivers' arrival in Yunnan—Chairman Mao Zedong declared that all urban students must "submit themselves to reeducation at the hands of the poor and lower middle peasants." Repercussions of the Great Helmsman's edict reverberated through Yunnan's borderlands:

Over the second half of 1969 a wave of *zhiqing* from Beijing, Shanghai, and Kunming flooded into Xishuangbanna. The Beijing contingent was dominated by those who had been first-and-second-year high school students in 1966. Some had still been in primary school. These little kids were good talkers. They would tell us straight off how their parents had been sent away to May Seventh Cadre Schools, how older brothers and sisters had gone up to the mountains and down to the villages. These kids had nobody to look after them. They typically dressed in blue Sun Yat-sen jackets or "army green." They rode around on bikes with bells on the handlebars. They would form gangs, get into fights, flash knives around. Or they would go to "pat down the ladies," that is, chat up the girls.

Shanghai *zhiqing* were rather taller, skin a bit whiter, and more sophisticated in the ways of the world. In the confined space of their dorms, they were always able to use a sheet of plastic to wall off a little space of their own. Nearly all the Beijing and Shanghai students had a small wooden luggage trunk next to their beds, about 90 centimeters wide and 60 high. They would raise these up with earthen bricks and drape a piece of flowered plastic over the top to make a night table or dressing table, on top of which they would arrange a few decorative objects and, in a few cases, topping it off with a sprinkling of scented lotion to give it an elegant touch. This was, in today's parlance, extremely "*petit bourgeois*."

They went out of their way to make themselves a bit more elegant than their Beijing and Kunming confreres. Shortly after arrival, not surprisingly, many fell ill or contracted skin inflammation from mosquito and insect bites. Though working together on the farms, old workers and *zhiqing* alike spoke their own local dialects. China's regional dialects were mutually comprehensible—with the singular exception of the Shanghai dialect, which was Greek to everyone. [Speakers of other "exotic" dialects such as Cantonese and Fujianese were rare among Yunnan's *zhiqing*.] Though most of the Shanghai-ers understood standard Mandarin, they preferred to speak their own patois, even in the presence of outsiders, making everyone feel highly uncomfortable.

After the Shanghai *zhiqing* arrived, "the scenery became more attractive" on the work teams. Outside the dorms of the Shanghai girls, you could always see their freshly washed designer panties and bras blowing in the wind.

Kunming *zhiqing* on the other hand, were, like the language they spoke, unaffected and unsophisticated.

THE FIFTY-FIVERS GET A BIT OF RESPECT

With the en masse arrival of *zhiqing* came a host of problems for our leaders. For one thing, they no longer could take the time and effort to subject us to criticism. So we "Old Beijingers" found our situation somewhat improved. On top of this, after Ling Yu died from illness brought on by overwork, the old workers and the "Old Sichuan" and "Old Kunming" *zhiqing* became more sympathetic toward us. Furthermore, since the Rebels had already seized power, political struggles became less intense, and the leaders treated us with diminished severity.

LIFE IN THE PROPAGANDA CORPS

For all that, the Fifty-fivers lost what little collective power they had accumulated when they were "scattered like grains of sand" by the Farm leaders. Peng Zhenge's memoir recalls, in vivid detail, the ups and downs of life after the dispersal:

One day in 1970 the leaders ordered me to take my flute and report to the Branch Farm Amateur Propaganda Corps. The corps, short on musicians, needed me to play. Having bonded with lots of people in Team Six, having made so many friends, and being aware that much of the Propaganda Corps agenda was spreading sectarian dogma on behalf of political factions, I was reluctant to go. But orders from above were matters of life or death and my name had already been removed from the Team Six roster.

The Branch Farm Propaganda Corps was an amateur group, organized as a production squad under Team Five. There were a dozen or so of us. The evening I arrived, a State Farm leader in charge of propaganda spoke: "Right now each of our six Branch Farms has formed a Mao Zedong Thought Propaganda Brigade. Every farm will prepare a number for a joint performance. Besides giving shows on the road, each will take part in a State Farm production." Suddenly he added in a threatening tone of voice, "If you want to do your job, go to it. If you don't, get the hell out!" He was clearly addressing his remarks to me.

Once the leader was gone, everyone came, exchanged some friendly words with me, and introduced themselves. The head of the troupe, Zhang Yuhao, was a year older than I, a Shandongese who had grown up in Kunming. Wearing a pair of thick glasses, he did not cut an imposing figure. Everyone called him "Zhang-the-Blind." His voice, however, was loud and clear. He was big and tall and treated people in a straightforward manner. He had volunteered to come to the East Wind Farm in 1963 after graduating middle school. He said it was he who had got me transferred to the Propaganda Corps. The head of propaganda for the State Farm, he informed me, was a high school teacher who had come from Kunming to defend the frontier, adding, "Take everything he says with a grain of salt."

Zhang Yuhao and I were the oldest members of the Propaganda Corps and we got along famously with each other. We subsequently became lifelong friends. I had just learned to smoke and the two of us would sit on the bed chain smoking and chatting into the night. He told me that he had grown up in Shandong during land reform. When his father was labeled a landlord, he was sent to Kunming to live with his aunt. After 1958, as the economy tanked, life in auntie's home became increasingly tenuous. So, in 1962, as soon as he had graduated from middle school, he voluntarily reported to Banna. Though only sixteen, he was full of enthusiasm and insisted on managing his own life. He soon became a model worker and a CYL member. He was particularly fond of writing and reciting poetry. It was he who wrote the lyrics to the propaganda corps' theme song, as well as other numbers. "Zhang-the-Blind" was a capable person, very competitive. Whether performing a task or producing a show, he always tried to outshine the others. He generally succeeded. We worked well under his command.

While broadening his circle of friends, Peng played multiple roles in the Propaganda Corps—musician, actor, organizer. You Hai, assigned to another Corps, composed songs and wrote scripts. "The alpha and omega of our dramatic productions," testifies You Hai, "was the thought of Chairman Mao":

Some people didn't understand and sat there with glazed eyes, totally clueless as to what we were doing. That is because the local people lived in an extremely closed-in world. The audience would stand there, including little kids with butts hanging out from the slits in the seats of their pants. It was very hard to address the needs of such an audience. Our principal productions were performed for the employees and workers of our military company, some of them *zhiqing* like us. We always got reviewed by these people on the pluses and minuses of our performances.

Figure 8.1. *Zhiqing* **Propaganda team. (Chen Xinzeng collection)**

THE ARMY TAKES OVER

In 1970 Xishuangbanna's State Farms became Military Farms—"Army Farms" for short. The official name was: The Chinese People's Liberation Army Yunnan Production Brigade: First Division. Division Headquarters was in Jinghong. Our East Wind State Farm was renamed the Second Regiment. Regimental Headquarters were in Damenglong. Team Five of the Qianziao Production Team became the Chinese People's Liberation Army Yunnan Production Brigade First Division. Second Regiment, Fifth Battalion, Company Five. With this change came a large number of active-duty army officers to serve as Company Commanders or Directors. The old civilian cadres had the word "Acting" added in front of the titles. The active-duty servicemen came from the Vietnam War battlefield. These battle-hardened veterans had served in Vietnam, Laos, Cambodia, and on the Ho Chi-Minh trail.

The army took class origin seriously. They made me an Acting Platoon Leader. Because of his problematic class origins, Zhang Yuhao was only made an Acting Assistant Platoon Leader. This saddened us, and during our evening smoke conversations, I took pains to console him.

By now everyone was quite familiar with the active military, people who had fought for ten years in Indochina. There was a Regimental Staff Officer named Guan. I got to know him when we put on our performance at regimental head-quarters. A Tianjin student soldier he said that, of the ten who joined up with him ten years earlier, he was the only one was left with all four limbs. One was confined to a wheelchair. All the others were dead.

For all its trials and tribulations, life in the countryside introduced the Fifty-five to social strata that they would never have gotten to know in Beijing. Peng appreciated his military friends:

Both retired and active-duty individuals had a bit of the ruffian in them tem-pered by a bit of humor. They weren't "decent, respectable" types of people. We referred to those who tried to act so upright and proper as "phonies." You didn't find in these old veterans the kind of short-fused temper that characterized the Rebel Faction.

Peng became a stalwart member of the Propaganda Corps, playing the lead role in the revolutionary opera "Taking Tiger Mountain by Strategy." He went out of his way to recruit other members of the Beijing contingent. After a whirlwind tour of revolutionary productions, however, the corps was broken up and returned to manual labor duties.

PRODUCTIVITY BLITZES

The backbone of Team Five were workers who had migrated from Hunan in 1960. Some of their rubber trees were already producing lactose. Propaganda Corps duties made us unavailable for the team's work and our late-to-bed late-to-rise production schedule engendered resentment.

Figure 8.2. Newly planted terraces of rubber trees. (Chen Xinzeng collection)

To boost morale, Peng joined with Zhang-the-Blind to mobilize for a Productivity Blitz—a crusade to clear, burn, and terrace new land. Blitzes took their team to an area of primeval forest where they built crude huts with bamboo sleeping platforms. During the first year they planted the newly cleared land. The peanut harvest took place on a stormy day. Though the crop grew moldy, peanuts, being classified as a staple, could not simply be given away, so they rotted in the warehouse.

Peng and his comrades were learning a lesson that would one day prove invaluable in pursuing official careers: Common sense must yield to bureaucratic imperatives. The following year the team constructed terraces and planted rubber. Teams cleared the slopes during the dry season to enable planting before the onset of the annual monsoon. This project promoted group solidarity, raising morale. The final day of the Blitz, just before the Chinese New Year, their leader "Zhang Dapao" ("Big Cannon Zhang") mobilized the entire battalion and threw them into the battle. Rising at 4 a.m., the Propaganda Corps worked through the day and into the night. For a celebratory feast, they slaughtered a pig and grooved on music from a semi-conductor radio.

A BEIJINGER ON THE RISE

Besides serving as Commander of the Propaganda Corps, I had also been appointed Acting Adjutant Company Commander. The current Battalion Political Commissar said to me, "Peng Zhenge, we are gathering outside information regarding your application for Party membership. As soon as we get a reply from your father and mother's work unit, we can resolve it without delay." Before long, our Company's Party branch held a meeting and approved my application. So simple, so quick. Not at all like the run-around I got when I applied to CYL.

Having arrived as idealistic but inexperienced youths, Peng and his comrades were maturing:

During my two or three years with the Propaganda Corps, I had grown into a dashing young man. I was twenty-four or twenty-five years old, strong of body and with a mind of my own. I was no longer an obedient child. And I had developed a smoking addiction.

BACK TO SCHOOL?

On an earlier home leave, Peng Zhenge had paid a visit to Liu Anzhang's father, a famous geologist. Academic acumen, Professor Liu informed him, diminished with age. At the time, the twenty-six-year-old Peng had not been in a classroom for half a dozen years. Now thirty, he was hospitalized, recovering from a work-related accident. Since Liu Anzhang was in the same hospital, recuperating from abdominal surgery, Peng's thoughts returned to a subject close to the hearts of millions of sent-down youth—how to resume a long-interrupted education. Serendipitously, a new policy had been proclaimed: Colleges might resume undergraduate recruitment. Only those of certified revolutionary class background, however, would be eligible to apply. These new hopefuls would be referred to as "Worker/Peasant/Soldier students":

> Each day my friend and I went over the material that they had prepared for the pre-Cultural-Revolution university entrance exams. But when we reviewed this stuff for the second time, it seemed even more familiar. Laboring in Xishuangbanna, it seemed, cleared the mind marvelously.

Once again, however, Cultural Revolutionary politics stifled youthful hopes. Zhang Tiesheng, a college applicant in the Northeast, had been proclaimed a national hero after submitting a blank examination booklet, claiming that he had been too busy making revolution to bother preparing. Peng ruefully recalls:

> Consequently, the culture-based exam was eliminated for the worker/peasant/ soldier students and one's entrance to the university became totally dependent upon the "recommendation of the masses," which meant, in practice, that your leaders had the final word. So neither Anyang nor I got into the university.

The vast majority of the Fifty-five never reentered the portals of academe. Like many disappointed and disillusioned sent-down youth, Peng reset his focus on doing what he could to incrementally improve life on China's southwestern frontier:

> The Fifth Battalion Propaganda Corps was dissolved. Together with Zhang-the-Blind, I got the remaining dozen or so members assigned to various maintenance or infrastructure construction companies. I was transferred to as a youth worker at Battalion Headquarters. When the Regiment Propaganda Corps needed me, I would go to help them stage productions.
>
> Half a year later I was made Director of the Regimental Propaganda Corps. My fellow student Zhong Yonghe was made Associate Director. The Corps had, by then, been relieved of production responsibilities.

Whether or not the Beijing Fifty-five would ever return to the nation's capital, they were at least finding opportunities to mitigate the tribulations of the Cultural Revolution and to contribute—however modestly—to life and culture on China's tropical frontier.

Chapter 9

Disillusionment

For young Beijing intellectuals self-exiled to a primitive frontier, disillusionment came not in a rushing torrent but in agonizing dribbles—a veritable "Chinese water torture." As You Hai recalled:

> When we first went to the countryside, everyone was really gung ho. We were convinced we could really make our mark, do something earth-shattering. But once we got down there, reality took over. You would find you couldn't get out of bed; you'd arrive late for meetings. After all, we were only human.
>
> It wasn't the torpid tropical lifestyle. It was just that we weren't the way we thought we were. People got sick, someone would have stomach problems and couldn't make the morning work detail. We had this notion that everyone should pull together, everyone should shoulder their hoe and bravely march up the mountain. In reality, we hadn't been there very long when everyone began to feel that this collective spirit was growing lax. The energy, it seemed, simply wasn't there; the will to do the job simply wasn't there.

In You Hai's diary, we see a *zhiqing*'s determination to keep the faith and hold fast to revolutionary convictions. In addition to bearing witness to daily struggles to survive on the frontier, she shows how events in faraway Beijing could challenge true believers seeking to process new information via the orthodox categories of revolutionary conformism. Most traumatic was the impending visit of President Richard Nixon in February 1972:

> Now this American—Nixon—is coming to our door to sue for peace. I am utterly mystified. Nixon, it would appear, is turning to peace negotiations in desperation because he has run out of options. With the clarion call of the anti-war movement, more and more Americans are coming to their senses. Abroad, they are getting more and more deeply bogged down in the Indochina conflict. Their battlefield losses have been even more than they were in Korea. The US monster has been stopped in its tracks by a nation of thirteen million. The Soviet revisionists are challenging them for world hegemony. Nixon has come to a dead end. But he needs only to approach our door and we welcome him. . . .

At stake are diametrically opposed principles. Taiwan is sacred territory belonging to the People's Republic of China. Those old Americans must completely withdraw. This is the foundation of any negotiations. The American imperialists cannot instantly transform themselves into Buddhas. We must entertain not the slightest illusions about them. We can only fight them and wipe out still more of them. . . .

How I yearn to emulate that woman warrior in the movie, to throw myself onto the battlefield and slaughter the enemy, to kill American soldiers with my own two hands. How wonderful that day would be!

While You Hai's understanding of life and politics on the East Wind State Farm had evolved, in keeping with the realities of daily life, her sloganistic understanding of the larger world—"ping pong diplomacy" notwithstanding—remained frozen in time:

We must put our foreign policy in order by studying Chairman Mao. Chairman Mao is wise, he is great. Starting with a tiny ping-pong ball he has achieved a great victory in our diplomatic line!

The friends of our great nation are growing more and more numerous!

Our people's friends cover the entire globe!

Proletariat of the world unite!

People of the world unite to defeat the American imperialists and all their running dogs!

Following this ideological ejaculation, You Hai's perspective on the rural scene reveals a cautious critic, aware of local issues but reluctant to get involved. This adulator of Chairman Mao must confront criticism that she is not loyal enough:

Fighting within the Seventh Company is not coincidental. There is conflict among several factions which have been stirring up the masses and playing upon the gullibility of some people, especially some non-proletarian elements that have wormed their way in. I don't want to plunge into the middle of this without careful thought, going off half-cocked and making a big show of myself.

Even as she gives voice to her views, You Hai struggles to be true to her convictions without damaging her image:

Today there was a Struggle against Capitalism, Criticize Revisionism meeting. I tried to keep a low profile and a low key, aiming to reconcile and unite, but some people said I was being too conciliatory toward class enemies.

I a rightist! I don't think so. I have done everything according to the instructions of Chairman Mao. I have not relied on my own emotions.

After another gathering, she remembers:

I sincerely and whole-heartedly submitted to the meeting's theme: Struggle Against Capitalism/Criticize Revisionism. I was proactive in recognizing my own faults. And yet this had exactly the opposite result from what I had expected. People stepped forward to struggle with me. Naturally I felt that what I had been saying was correct. If we were going to struggle, let's get on with it, but we must maintain discipline. On this my convictions are inalterable.

In dealing with the faction-ridden world of rural Xishuangbanna, *zhiqing* faced an unending struggle to reaffirm revolutionary credentials without abandoning tactical pragmatism. Even as she recalled the song that the Fifty-fivers had sung as they embarked on their mission—"Stride Forth to Meet the Dawn"—and their oath—"Our hearts ever Red, our wills unshakable," You Hai faced challenges, not only from local leaders and activists but from fellow sent-down youth as well. Having spent years mentoring waves of new *zhiqing* from Chongqing, Kunming, and Shanghai, Beijing's Fifty-fivers still confronted a cultural divide. She found a

complex situation among *zhiqing*. Some people have a strong mentality peculiar to their native places. They are trying to form tight-knit bonds based upon sworn brotherhoods, more appropriate to feudalism or capitalism.

On September 6, 1971, the Party committee confirmed its confidence in You Hai by authorizing her to organize a new Company. When she sought medical treatment in Beijing, however, she was chastised for evading responsibilities. Whatever the difficulties, You resolved to shoulder her new duties and plunge ahead. Two days after taking on her new assignment, however, she could only "deeply regret that I am not a man." Besides being vulnerable to sexual exploitation at the hands of their political superiors, women *zhiqing* were compelled to prove their worth while laboring in the shadow of China's patriarchal culture.

Beijing politics, moreover, reverberated on the distant frontier: a nationwide witch hunt for conspirators in "the May Sixteenth counter-revolutionary plot"—a nationwide witch hunt that reached into the bosom of You Hai's own family:

My father was labeled a member of the May Sixteenth conspiracy. My mother was locked up. My parents were separated. Father was in a cowshed, Mother in a military work brigade. Every day they cross-examined my mother, trying to get her to confess to being a member of the May Sixteenth conspiracy. Finally, they said, if you don't cooperate, we'll throw you and your husband into prison and your children will never see you again. My mother ultimately admitted that she was a May Sixteener and so was my father. Father eventually died in a rage because Mother had betrayed him.

I finally came to my senses. When I returned to Beijing and saw Father and Mother, I cried bitterly. From this point on I began to understand. After that I reflected deeply on things.

Whatever happened to families in faraway Beijing, You and her comrades had to live their lives on the East Wind Farm in Xishuangbanna. Only an event of cosmic proportions could begin to erode foundations of their revolutionary commitment.

THE DEATH OF LIN BIAO

In April 1969, Minister of Defense Lin Biao had been officially designated Mao Zedong's "closest comrade-in-arms and successor." Unlike Mao, Lin had little personal charisma and, outside of the military, no independent base of support. Nonetheless, the promise that the nation could anticipate a constitutionally legitimated revolutionary successor totally devoted to Mao and his vision assured the nation that the radical policies of the Cultural Revolution—including the "sending down" of educated youth—might well continue indefinitely.

Together with Chairman Mao, Lin Biao was expected to appear on the Gate of Heavenly Peace to preside over the October 1, 1971, National Day celebration. After the event was abruptly canceled, word spread through Party channels that Lin, together with his wife and son, had died in a September 13 plane crash while fleeing to the Soviet Union after plotting, unsuccessfully, to assassinate Mao.

Thanks to well-connected families in China's capital, many Fifty-fivers kept politically informed. Through word of mouth and letters from home, accounts of events routinely filtered down to Xishuangbanna. Word of Lin's apostasy and demise, however, came like a bolt from the blue. Returning from home leave, Peng Zhenge was happily sharing with fellow students gossip he had heard in Beijing—as well as the food he had brought back—when he heard someone exclaim, "Lin Biao is dead!"

Within weeks, the shocking news had become common knowledge. Until officially announced, however, these things could be discussed only *sotto voce* with close friends. Once word of the Lin affair, disseminated through Party channels, had made its way to the State Farm, an authorized version of events was conveyed through a month-long series of public meetings. Finally, the official document reached the Fifth Company of the Fifth Battalion and the entire Production Company was summoned to the drill field. When it came to the part about Lin Biao betraying Mao and dying on a plane crash in Mongolia, some of the young women broke down. Hadn't Lin only recently been proclaimed a minor deity?

By this time, some Fifty-fivers were already entertaining second thoughts about their commitment to living out their lives as manual laborers on China's southwest frontier. Beginning with Wang Xiaoyun, a general's daughter who had used her father's connections to enlist in the military, a handful had already found ways out.

Interviewed some thirty years later, few Fifty-five mentioned the Lin Biao affair. A prominent exception is Li Zhenzhan, the most politically promising member of the group, whose meteoric rise had been jump-started by the Cultural Revolution:

> It was the Lin Biao incident that really had the greatest impression on me. Nobody had imagined that somebody to whom we had all wished long life on a daily basis could end up like this.

Most striking is the testimony of Yin Zheng, who had stalwartly put aside ideological issues to focus on the tasks before him:

> The crash of Lin Biao's plane produced widespread reverberations. One of the goals of the CR had been to set up Lin Biao as Mao's successor. Suddenly we saw we had been taken for suckers. We also felt that the whole rustification movement was a fraud. So, from that moment on, thoughts of returning to the city became powerful.

As an isolated incident, the Lin Biao affair could scarcely turn true believers into skeptics or cynics. Struggling to cope with life on a frontier farm, the Fifty-five could scarcely allow themselves to be distracted by far-off events, no matter how dramatic. Though the Lin Biao dénouement, in and of itself, could not precipitate a crisis of values, it did, however, as Yin Zheng testifies, erode foundations of faith, vitiate revolutionary commitments, and accelerate a desire to return home:

> The affair didn't lead to a disbelief in everything, but I did feel that I could no longer go along believing all I heard without critical appraisal.

You Hai recalls how the pervasive sense of disillusionment and betrayal provoked her to reexamine her entire *zhiqing* experience:

> After the May Sixteenth thing and the Lin Biao incident, my mind began to see things clearly. I felt I had let myself get taken in.

On a national level, Lin Biao's death marked a watershed in the Cultural Revolution. A movement that had initially combined social mobilization with reconfiguration of China's power structure now focused on the microcosm of court politics, as individuals and factions jockeyed to seize power after the passing of an aging Chairman Mao. Byzantine intrigues in Beijing eventually reshaped the political and ideological barriers walling in the Beijing Fifty-five.

While Lin Biao's anointment in the late 1960s had presaged the realization of the Maoist vision, Deng Xiaoping's resurrection in the mid-1970s underscored the need to restore order. Exiled to a provincial factory after being labeled "the number two person in power following the capitalist road," Deng reemerged in China's capital to help reunify the Party under the moderating influence of Premier Zhou Enlai.

One effort to mitigate the excesses of the Cultural Revolution was the reopening of universities and admission of "worker-peasant-soldier" students in the early 1970s. Assuming that rural labor qualified them as "workers," if not as "peasants," some Fifty-fivers sought college admission under the new regulations, only to find available slots allotted to applicants with family ties or political connections to local cadres. Reborn aspirations for higher education nonetheless reminded them of their identity as aspiring intellectuals and spurred them to register for after entrance exams provisionally reinstituted in December 1977 and made permanent in June 1978.

Bizarre though it might have been to link together a Communist renegade Lin Biao with a vilified sage, the "Criticize Confucius Criticize Lin Biao" movement that played itself out from 1973 to 1976 brought about unintended consequences. For culturally deprived Beijingers-in-exile, it offered reassurance that it was OK to read books. The Cultural Revolution—anti-intellectual to its core—had popularized a belief that everything worth knowing would be found in the selected works of the Chairman or in pithy words of Maoist wisdom quoted in the catechistic *Little Red Book*. But to criticize Confucius, one had to return to the Chinese classics. And to criticize Lin Biao, it was useful to read the Marxist literature.

For You Heng, the message was clear. Only by returning to the classroom could she maximize her potential contribution to her nation:

I don't like the argument that "We should settle in here for life." So far as getting along goes, I can't help but play my role, but I only have one thought: to continue my schooling, to continue to study, so as to prepare myself properly for the long-term struggle. Why is this so bad? To learn something new is not for my personal benefit but to enable me to give everything I can to my native land! What's not to like?

Five months later, however, as hopes remained unfulfilled, You Hai's mood turned darker:

The sky is leaden. Black clouds loom on the horizon.

I am shouldering my hoe, trudging on with heavy steps, slowly walking down the grey road. Grass has grown tall over the graves and the earth seems to have fallen down of its own weight. Time slips by so slowly. Before me I still seem to see the long, emaciated, shadow of myself. . . .

My thoughts have gone off track, that bright and shining road that summons me. I have always thought that I had nothing to be ashamed of in this life and that after death my brave soul would remain immortal. But "flowers bud and bloom, petals fade and fall." In a single step, in the twinkling of the eye, it's all over. You disappear from the scene without a sound, without a sigh. . . . See reality for what it is; don't flinch. Escape is for the weak-minded, suicide for the coward. The only way for anyone with the courage of her own convictions is to struggle.

Looking down that murky road, listening to the chirping of the birds, brings back the breath of life, and I rediscover my inner strength. The road still breathes life. Despair vanishes. Focus on my studies.

My heart is heavy and ill at ease. Should I blame myself? No. Reality is speaking. If you don't respect reality, how can you talk about materialism?

I continue along my path toward the "grave." I only hope that I can go to an ordinary death after living an extraordinary life.

Nearly a fortnight later, on November 21, 1973, she seizes hope from the jaws of despair:

If we hadn't decided to go down to the grassroots, if we hadn't gone through this turbulent experience, we would never be able to understand why things are the way they are. Looking ahead to our future, I am convinced that this kind of experience is a big plus.

One might think she had been reading Voltaire—

"Pangloss sometimes said to Candide:

'There is a concatenation of events in this best of all possible worlds: for if you had not been kicked out of a magnificent castle for love of Miss Cunegonde: if you had not been put into the Inquisition: if you had not walked over America:

if you had not stabbed the Baron: if you had not lost all your sheep from the fine country of El Dorado: you would not be here eating preserved citrons and pistachio-nuts.'

'All that is very well,' answered Candide, 'but let us cultivate our garden.'"

For now, they were trapped on the Farm. The garden that awaited them was far away—in Beijing.

Chapter 10

Back to Beijing

Driven by collective commitment, the Fifty-five had come to the State Farm as a group. As dedication gave way to disillusionment, they left the frontier to return to Beijing one by one, each seeking his or her individual fortune. The strategy: persuade local officials to authorize the transfer of residency permits, then use hometown connections to find jobs.

The first Fifty-fiver departed in 1971. Li Man, an intrepid activist in the "Majority Faction," had found life increasingly frustrating under the Farm's autocratic military leaders. With the help of Zeng Silai's father (a PLA general), Li was able to pull strings and join the army.

Other Fifty-fivers from politically prominent families found fathers and mothers on the receiving end of the Cultural Revolution, packed off to rural labor camps euphemistically dubbed "May 7th Schools." Only a fortunate few managed to get transferred back to Beijing. One, with a father fallen gravely ill and siblings too young to shoulder family responsibilities, returned home thanks to permission from a sympathetic commander. Another young man, who had returned to Beijing to treat an abdominal illness, found himself legally barred from remaining there. Rather than return to the Farm, he moved to a mountainous area in nearby Shanxi where his mother had connections from her wartime service in Mao's Eighth Route army.

Even the process of returning from home leave could be complicated. In 1973, Chen Jinsheng—who had been in Beijing for more than a year undergoing medical procedures—bid farewell to an old schoolmate who had come along to take care of him. "Even if you don't go back to the Farm, I'm leaving," announced his friend. "Now there will be nobody to take care of you. Let me arrange for you to be permanently returned home for medical reasons." Chen demurred: "Even if I get relocated because of my physical condition, I won't have a salary. How can I manage to live here?" Chen eventually returned to the Farm, where a well-connected friend arranged for his release on grounds of health. His benefactor's parting words: "Get the hell out of here!"

Challenges could be especially daunting when medical crises were exacer-
bated by family disasters. As one recalled:

> My liver disease reoccurred. I was not in good shape. I began treatment for
> my illness during my 1971 home leave. My father was already in the "cadre
> school," having been labeled a traitor. My family situation was really depress-
> ing. And my mother had severe heart problems. There was nobody at home to
> take charge since my younger brother was also a village *zhiqing*. I was in dire
> straits. At first I returned to the Farm because I felt conscientiously compelled to
> do so. After I left, my mother had another life-threatening attack. In 1971 I went
> on a home visit. I finally got my residence permit transferred back to Beijing.

A handful of Fifty-fivers who had managed to launch political careers in
Yunnan felt less urgency about returning home. Minority faction leaders He
Longkang and his wife, Liang Bangmei, remained in Yunnan into the early
1990s; he winning a key position in the Labor Ministry's Office of Science
and Technology, and she in the Standing Committee of the Yunnan People's
Congress. Availing themselves of official connections, they were eventually
able to continue careers in the nation's capital.

Several managed to parlay intellectual backgrounds into teaching positions
in local schools. Some got assigned to technical posts. Still others moved
into low- and mid-level positions in the farm bureaucracy. Even members of
the majority faction sometimes fared well—providing they eschewed frontal
confrontation and offered usable political skills. One, transferred in 1974 to a
provincial office in Kunming, was joined, in 1977, by a Fifty-fiver comrade
whom he had married the previous year. Nearly everybody, including those
assigned to office jobs, labored, at least part time, under the merciless tropical
sun, felling forests and planting groves of rubber trees.

Strings pulled in the nation's capital did not necessarily resonate in
Xishuangbanna. On one occasion, a sympathetic official in Beijing's Bureau
of Sent-down Youth garnered State Council approval to bring back individuals qualified to serve as teachers. When hopeful Fifty-fivers sought to enroll
in this program, however, a farm leader declared: "I kowtow to no one. My
word is law." The head of the local Sent-down Youth Office minced no words
as he gloated: "I've got you trapped in Yunnan."

A Beijing exile might, with a bit of luck, find a sympathetic ear. One young
woman setting out for family leave received these parting words of friendly
advice from a battalion commander, himself a transferred-down northern
official: "Don't return until you have found a marriage partner in Beijing." He
understood that only a certificate of matrimony could open a path for escape.
When she reemerged, still unattached, he exclaimed:

What? You're back again? I know you have the best of intentions, but, think about it. What kinds of people are we down here in this mountain ravine? What kind of people are those guys up there? They are Beijingers. They are five thousand miles away. How can they even find us?

Even as disillusionment and cynicism became more widespread, the Fifty-fivers struggled to survive, both physically and spiritually. On January 20, 1976, as the Chinese New Year approached, Wang Kaiping loaded a tractor with sugar cane and drove it back to share with his work team in a holiday celebration. When the tractor stalled while climbing a steep slope, Wang leaped off and started pushing from behind. The tractor overturned, crushing him to death. To make matters worse, local officials refused to honor him as a martyr who had given his life for his comrades. Rather, they belittled him for going off to find luxuries for himself and his friends when he should have been planting rubber trees. The incident drove one more nail into the Fifty-fivers' coffin of despair.

By the time Mao died, in September 1976, the oldest of the Fifty-five was nearly thirty. Even the youngest had passed the age at which—but for the Cultural Revolution—they should have been comfortably settled with spouses, children, and official positions in China's capital. By this time, desperation to go home was all but universal.

Vicissitudes in high-level leadership, however, did little more than fine-tune the policy of sending young urbanites to the countryside. Lin Biao—Mao's designated successor and comrade-in-arms—had died after an attempted coup. With Zhou Enlai's star on the rise, the moderate Deng Xiaoping had returned to Beijing. Then Zhou had died and Deng had fallen into disgrace. Following Mao's passing and the arrest of his wife and her ultra-leftist comrades, "The Gang of Four," Mao's successor, Hua Guofeng had discretely toned down some of the Great Leader's more radical policies. Through all of this, the Sent-Down-Youth program remained in place.

Not until 1978 did new forces emerge to break the logjam. In December, at the Third Plenum of the Eleventh Central Committee, Deng Xiaoping positioned himself to challenge Hua Guofeng's leadership, proclaiming an era of reform. Even before Deng's ascension, a group of *zhiqing* on Yunnan's state farms had raised a banner for return to the cities. Driving the movement were sent-down youth from Shanghai; Beijing's Fifty-Fivers were conspicuously sidelined. Yunnan had, in any event, become a launching pad for nationwide resistance.

By 1978, China's leaders generally acknowledged that a reassessment of the Sent-Down movement was overdue. However, outright reversal of a policy anointed by Mao Zedong remained unthinkable. While abandoning wholesale rustification, reforms left in place those trapped in remote villages and on state farms.

Once changes came, they were swift and far-reaching. By 1979 *zhiqing* from far-flung reaches of rural China were returning to the cities en masse. By 1980 the Fifty-five had, with few exceptions, decamped to Beijing. Only a handful who had managed to secure provincial appointments or gain admission to local institutions of higher education remained in Kunming. Within a few years, they too had left.

Returnees were woefully unprepared for what awaited them. Now in their late twenties and early thirties, lacking university or, in most cases, even high school diplomas, they were hardly positioned to compete with a younger, newly educated cohort. The China of Mao Zedong in which they had been born, raised, and politically socialized was crumbling under their feet. In its place the China of Deng Xiaoping was embarking upon an uncharted course of reform. The great enterprise to which they had pledged their futures lay in ruins. How could the Fifty-five bring order and purpose to their own lives, let alone help to rebuild their traumatized nation?

Chapter 11

Conclusion

Finding the Lost Generation

How, within a few short years, did China transform itself from the basket case of Cultural Revolution to the success story of Reform? The official explanation has been that all good things materialized thanks to enlightened policies of the CCP under a series of visionary leaders: Deng Xiaoping, Jiang Zemin, Hu Jintao, and Xi Jinping. (With Xi elevated to imperial status, his Reform Era antecedents have now been all but forgotten.) Without denying the importance of top-level leadership, stories of the Fifty-five show that China's dramatic transformation owes much to individuals in the middle echelons—not to mention, of course, the hard work of ordinary people.

In recent interviews with some dozen recently retired Fifty-fivers, I encountered several who, having returned to Beijing following a decade of labor on the Yunnan frontier, navigated the treacherous currents of the reform era to make signal contributions to China's rebirth. Their stories suggest that the "Lost Generation" of sent-down youths was not entirely lost.

Least surprising among the Fifty-fivers' success stories was that of Yin Zheng. Having gained renown as a model worker, Yin secured permission to study computer science at Shanghai's renowned Fudan University. He subsequently rose to the rank of Senior Colonel in the Chinese Air Force. When I interviewed "Iron Man Yin" in 2002, he declined to discuss details of his military career, apparently because of his high security status. He did not hesitate, however, to share philosophical and political views. Yin's no-nonsense work ethic and contempt for ideology were, if anything, even more pronounced than they had been in his youth. He was highly critical of Mao Zedong, comparing China under his rule to present-day North Korea. In contrast to Chinese obsession with power, he found Americans admirably practical and apolitical. Yin Zheng's ideal ruler was George Washington, who refused to transform himself from Father of the Revolution to King of the Republic.

Figure 11.1. Yin Zheng celebrates a birthday. (Author's collection)

Before we parted, Yin invited me to return in twenty years, when he might be able to share details of his military career. "By that time," I demurred, "I will be eighty-seven and will have to visit you in a wheelchair." I now find myself a still-ambulant eighty-seven-year-old, but Iron Man Yin Zheng has been dead for sixteen years. If he left behind like-minded comrades in the ranks of the PLA, we are unlikely to hear from them.

I became acutely aware of the Fifty-fivers' ability to adapt to the new era in another 2002 interview, this one with seaside resort manager Li Zhenzhan. Son of a Xinjiang worker who had moved to Beijing with his widowed mother, Li had ridden the Cultural Revolutionary wave to parlay a working-class background into a political career.

One of the few Fifty-fivers who could claim to be a progeny of the proletariat, Li Zhenzhan's ties to Beijing were shallower than those of his fellow students, having arrived only recently from Xinjiang. Once in the countryside, he joined the Fifty-five's Minority Faction, which decried criticism of local leaders and policies as manifestations of urban bourgeois arrogance. His class background and politically correct beliefs were soon rewarded.

Raising the banner of "Never forget class struggle," Li exuded fulsome praise for veteran workers who tutored the Fifty-five in the rudiments of agricultural work and joined hands to "expose the counter-revolutionary conspiracy of a handful of class enemies" whom he blamed for a "criminal conspiracy to subvert the dictatorship of the proletariat and restore capitalism." In July

Figure 11.2. The author with Li Zhenzhan, Guangdong, 2002. (Author's collection)

1969, the young stalwart was placed on the farm's Provincial Revolutionary Committee. Soon afterward, he was elevated to Company Commander—to which he added the title of Branch Party Secretary. In 1973 Li Zhenzhan joined Chairman Mao on the rostrum of Beijing's Gate of Heavenly Peace.

With the abrupt shift of political winds after the Chairman's death and the downfall of the ultra-Maoist Gang of Four, Li's fortunes plummeted. Following the launching of reforms in the early 1980s, however, he reemerged in Shenzhen, a boomtown on China's capitalist-tinged southern frontier. There he had parlayed political skills into a successful career—just as he had done under very different circumstances during the Cultural Revolution.

I found Li living very much in the present. Fifty-fivers' struggles between the majority and minority factions, he claimed, were insignificant since most protagonists had long since buried the hatchet. The Cultural Revolution? Past history! We must eschew judgments about what was good and bad.

What sins had Li committed, I asked, to bring retribution upon his head after the fall of the Gang of Four? His answer: He had done what everybody else did—toed the official line. Here was a man who wanted to be judged on his accomplishments—not on how he achieved them. The only political assessment he would offer was that he still considered Mao Zedong a great man. Scarcely a sentiment likely to get him into trouble.

Li portrayed himself as someone who got results. A tour of the grounds showed that he had mastered the marketplace of reform just as deftly as he had surfed the tides of the Cultural Revolution. At a time when only a favored few had access to automobiles, clients arrived at his resort in late-model limousines, symbols of membership in the official-commercial elite. To serve their needs, Li maintained relations with local power brokers, employing skills honed on the Yunnan frontier. Li still viewed himself as a visionary—but as one whose visions could now be translated into realities:

> When I was young, I dreamed of the emancipation of the whole human race, to transform heaven and earth, to temper myself to be eternally loyal to the Party and Chairman Mao. But those youthful dreams were vast and hazy. The ones I have now are down to earth.

That statement could serve as the logo for his generation.

In 2018 I visited another resort town—Anning—site of Yunnan's famous hot springs—to interview Li Daling. Li recalled a career trajectory unequalled by any of his erstwhile comrades. Having attended the elite No. 25 High School, along with China's current President Xi Jinping, and having shared Xi's aspiration to pursue a degree at Tsinghua University (China's MIT), Li had found himself—like Xi and seventeen million others—consigned to manual labor in the hinterland. Like Xi, Li Daling had ferreted out opportunities in the provinces and in the capital. Launching his career without Xi's family and Party connections, Li had retired politically powerless but financially well-heeled, with a high level of personal satisfaction and a cosmopolitan worldview. His career suggests that historical forces paving the way for a Xi Jinping to rule China from above also offered opportunities for less famous sent-down youth to build institutions from the bottom up.

For Li, like Xi, experience in the countryside had itself been an education. In the course of this decade, he had acquired an experientially based understanding of his country and the ability to negotiate an endlessly changing succession of challenges, drawing upon interpersonal skills appropriate for dealing with diverse strata of society.

Thanks to his educational prowess in the sciences and math, Li discovered ample outlets for talents. He found himself assigned to an engineering company, where he mastered lumbering and construction. While making his mark as a manual laborer, young Li emerged as a daring innovator, advancing through the ranks of the local Communist apparatus. Asked to consolidate Party organization at the East Wind Farm's hospital, he recalls dashing forward "like a newborn calf that has not yet learned to fear the tiger."

Soon after Li's arrival at the hospital, when a Dai woman succumbed to terminal cancer, fellow villagers stormed the gates seeking revenge against her doctor. Facing down the enraged crowd, Li had persuaded them to send a few representatives into the operating room. There, this transplanted young urbanite totally devoid of medical experience had grabbed a scalpel, slit open the cadaver's abdomen, and revealed the toxic sea of the cancerous cells that had killed the patient. The room fell silent. "OK," said Li, "sew her up again and give her a proper burial. We have done our duty."

Though a proposal to train him as a physician failed to gain traction, young Li had become a rising star. Placed in charge of a production unit with more than a hundred people, he had confronted "ultra-leftist" cadres who had been vilified as "capitalist roaders"—farmers who had dared to raise a few chickens or pigs. Li went on to persuade Battalion Headquarters to issue boots to parents and children who trekked barefoot through fields fertilized by human waste. His efforts helped ensure a reliable source of vegetables to feed fellow workers. To counter critics who denounced profit-motivated enterprises in the name of ideological purity, Li flaunted the Marxist mantra: "Revolution Is Nothing More Than Liberating the Forces of Production!" Critics scowled, but his policies prevailed.

Looking back, Li traces his success as a pragmatic frontier reformer to the experience of growing up in Beijing. Raised by hard-strapped parents from rural and military backgrounds, he had spent middle and high school summer holidays as a volunteer laborer in poor mountain villages. When friends in the Yunnan countryside asked him why he always smiled, even while living in a thatched hut, he had replied that he relished "eating bitterness" as one more "toughening up" experience.

By the late 1970s, Li was well situated to take advantage of higher educational opportunities that materialized as Cultural Revolutionary icon Mao Zedong sickened and died. While his old schoolmate Xi Jinping won admission to Tsinghua, Li, now a young husband and father, applied to the premier higher educational institution in his underdeveloped province. When Yunnan University's economic department found this brilliant and resilient sent-down youth knocking on the door of its admissions office, it had unhesitatingly ushered him in. Li's teachers were not to be disappointed. Upon graduation in 1982, he was appointed instructor—even though he had taken not a single graduate-level course.

Li's plans for advanced study were cut short by an offer from Beijing's Export-Import Bank. Though a rising provincial star, he realized that a chance to work in Beijing for a key player in his chosen field of international monetary policy was too good to pass up. Relocated to China's capital, Li devoted his efforts to bring China into the international business community—a key plank of Deng Xiaoping's reform agenda. In the mid-1980s he led a delegation of young bankers to Holland for a two-month training course during which he negotiated international monetary issues on behalf of his bank.

To his dismay, Li returned to his Beijing to find his office riven by rivalries among newcomers seeking to compensate for lost time in the countryside by clawing their way up the organizational ladder. Disheartened by power struggles, he began to reassess professional options. Before long, the opportunity he had been seeking arrived at his doorstep—an introduction to Wang Qishan, vice-governor of the China Construction Bank.

Wang's meteoric career took him to Guangdong province; Li went with him. Soon he was running the provincial office of the Chinese Rural Investment Bank. On the frontier of economic reform adjacent to Hong Kong, Li put his talents to work. When his mentor's Guangdong operation fell victim to political infighting, however, he found it impossible to continue. Availing himself of contacts in adjacent Hainan, he was now authorized to convert a state-run investment company into a shareholding corporation. Having established a regional reputation, Li relocated to a neighboring province to pilot the Hainan Development Bank, an official investment firm run on the new shareholder model. When managerial problems erupted, however, Premier Zhu Rongji unleashed a torrent of top-to-bottom audits that left Li exhausted and dispirited.

Already a recognized administrative entrepreneur in the hot field of investment banking, Li went on to found Huarong Investment Ltd. Two decades later, he returned, successful and wealthy, to Beijing, where he was declared a "high level human resource," making him eligible for retirement income while retaining his official title. Gradually gearing down professional activities, Li spent his final years of service easing into full retirement, residing alternately in his Beijing apartment and on his Hainan estate.

By the time of our 2018 interview, seventy-three-year-old Li was living in his second retreat, a glistening three-story residence in Anning. Now separated from his wife, he had visited more than forty foreign countries, starting with official junkets, moving on to group tourism, and finally morphing into independent travel in the company of intimate friends.

Survival skills tested in Yunnan and honed through years in investment banking served Mr. Li well during trips abroad. Golden Eagle pass in hand, he and friends rented a camper to explore America's national parks. Though a foreign tourist speaking limited English, Li finessed a highway patrol run-in with survival skills that had served him well during his sent-down youth and challenging career. A trooper who had pulled him over for making an illegal left turn while ferreting out a remote Chinese buffet, ended up, red lights flashing, guiding the vanload of Chinese visitors to their luncheon destination.

Having negotiated the treacherous currents of Reform and Opening Up, Li sees his country with hope but few illusions: "We have already accomplished much, but the path has been tortuous. From start to finish, I have never retreated but have continued to move forward and have never been stopped in my tracks by a new setback." Li hoped to continue to travel, to explore, to enjoy life. If physical infirmities limited his activities, he would simply stop eating and die. Otherwise, he hoped to live to 120.

Zhang Xinhui followed his own path to success in post-Maoist China. Son of working-class parents, Zhang boasted the kind of "good" family background that opened doors in China's class-conscious socialist order. Schoolmates at the No. 5 High School included scions of high officials. Enhancing his favorable class status, Zhang displayed political skills that propelled him to leadership in the school's Communist Youth League.

When the Cultural Revolution broke out, Zhang was a member of what came to be known as the "Old Red Guards"—students from cadre and worker families who had launched the movement. Soon, however, these activists found themselves challenged by a rival faction taking cues from Mao's personal directives rather than from the Party and the CYL. Proclaiming that "It's right to rebel," the radicals' "Rebel Faction"—dominated by students with intellectual, urban bourgeois, and other less favored backgrounds—vilified rivals as ersatz revolutionaries. In defense, Zhang and his comrades flaunted their politically correct family origins. Their logo: "If dad is a hero, the son is a great guy. If dad is a counter-revolutionary, the son is an SOB."

With schools closed, factional rivalry turned lethal, and China's cities careening toward chaos, Zhang and his peers, sought a way out. Following a stint of voluntary factory labor, he joined the movement to "exchange revolutionary experiences," traveling by train and on foot across the map of China. His moment of truth came during a visit to an orphanage in the northwest province of Xikang, where he found hundreds of children whose parents had starved to death during what had been officially proclaimed the "three years of natural disaster" (1959–1962). Though Beijingers had endured widespread belt-tightening during these difficult times, he only now realized that rural compatriots had faced starvation. Shaken by cognitive dissonance, moral angst, and the prospect of a chaotic and undefined future in the nation's capital, Zhang seized the chance to build a rubber industry on the southwest frontier.

In Yunnan, Zhang further honed his survival skills. When the Fifty-five were dispersed to branch farms, he assumed a leadership role in his new location. While a rising star in the local Party organization, Zhang became aware of realities that belied official nostrums about the nobility of the working class, slogans he had loyally parroted since primary school. As leaders on the State Farm, these presumed paragons of the proletariat had revealed themselves to be ruthless self-serving opportunists. In daily lives, paragons of the working class relentlessly struggled for self-advantage and engaged in the kinds of marital infidelity that Zhang had been taught to associate with a corrupt ruling elite.

One of the last Fifty-fivers to return home, Zhang reemerged in Beijing a thirty-year-old, married, with child, and without career prospects. To make matters worse, China's inflexible residency regulations separated him from his wife and son. Rather than join Zhang in Beijing, his spouse, infant son in arms, had been forced to relocate to Shanghai, her registered hometown.

What saved Zhang were well-honed survival skills. When his mother retired from her lower-level managerial post in the garment industry, he was able to fill her slot, though as an ordinary fabric cutter. Freed of family responsibilities, he simultaneously enrolled in a part-time economic management curriculum at the neighborhood People's University's correspondence school, emerging three years later with a certificate, though no diploma.

Now joined by family, his wife having swapped jobs with a Shanghai-er stranded in the capital, Zhang was entrusted with conducting on-the-job employee training. Promoted to assistant manager in charge of marketing, he found himself on the fast track toward higher management. With a delegation to Toronto, he spent four months absorbing lessons from the capitalist world's clothing industry. Back in Beijing, Zhang rose through Huabiao ranks to become Party Secretary and, in 1990, company CEO.

Since 1956, Huabiao Haberdashery had outfitted China's elite. The "Maosuit" in the Chairman's portrait on the Gate of Heavenly Peace is a Huabiao product—as is the button-in-the-back outfit that clads the Late Chairman's body in the Mao Mausoleum. Besides clothing national leaders, Huabiao tailored suits and ties for Foreign Ministry representatives and others headed abroad on official business, as well as for foreign embassy personnel in Beijing.

In Toronto, Zhang and his colleagues learned how to adapt their operation to a consumer market. In addition to mastering industry nuts and bolts, they realized that customers were interested in more than the goods they set out to purchase. Buyers shopped for confirmation of personal status, a phenomenon conveyed through the neologism "intangible assets."

Besides gaining an expansive concept of the clothing business, Zhang had brought home images of a brave new world—not only of ribbons of expressways but of a driver who slowed down to stick his head out the window and alert a woman in an adjacent car that her dress was caught in the door. He vividly recalled a Good Samaritan dropping heavy shopping bags on a Toronto sidewalk to guide a Chinese stranger to his destination. He had returned from his first trip abroad with both a roadmap for building a profitable business and an appreciation of foreign standards for social behavior.

Zhang was convinced that China needed to catch up with the West, not only in economic development but in ethical awareness. From an incident in a department store, he also learned a lesson that would serve him well in building a brand name. Informed that his elegant handmade cashmere coat would command only half the price of its Canadian counterpart because it carried a "made-in-China" label, he realized just how fast he and his fellow countrymen had to run if they were to catch up.

Equipping Huabiao to compete in the international marketplace was a tall order for a man whose youthful horizons had been hemmed in by the Xishuangbanna's mountains. After investing heavily in machinery necessary to meet the demands of seemingly insatiable domestic consumers, Zhang found his company struggling to unload surplus goods in a voraciously competitive market. Operating under state controls, he and his colleagues also realized how challenging it was to compete while underwriting welfare benefits dictated by China's socialist economy. Even in the Reform era, employers were required to assume full financial responsibility for financing worker unemployment and retirement. In addition, Huabiao had to take under its own roof less profitable state-run textile enterprises. Socialist values handicapped competitors in a capitalist marketplace.

In any event, Zhang relentlessly plunged ahead, determined to promote the Hongdu brand name in this challenging environment. He eventually concluded that he could succeed only by restructuring his state-controlled enterprise as a joint-stock company. A year's struggle, however, ended with an edict from above: He would have to confine reformist initiatives to the tightly circumscribed state enterprise framework. The CEO would be compelled to divide his efforts between meeting marketplace demands and conforming to official dictates.

Facing the prospect of unending struggle for uncertain results, Zhang resigned. Zhang was not the only Chinese who left the confined but secure world of a socialist economy for the enticing but uncertain rewards of the marketplace—a trend called "jumping into the sea." However, he took the plunge with a life preserver, remaining, though without an administrative position, on the Hong Du company roster. His monthly salary of some four or five thousand yuan was reduced to one thousand.

Widely recognized for his knowledge, experience, and adaptability, Zhang soon found a job managing and marketing for a friend who made Western musical instruments. Eventually, however, he accepted an offer to return to his old company where he continued as CEO until 2009, when he reached sixty—the mandated age for official retirement. Monthly income was now a modest three thousand yuan.

Watching from the sidelines a decade later, Zhang could see some of his efforts reaching fruition. In addition to official salaries, high-level management personnel were now rewarded with a portion of profits. For all his efforts, however, Zhang had to content himself with an inflation-adjusted monthly income of five thousand yuan. His and his wife's real wealth was in Beijing apartments, purchased from their work units some thirty years ago.

At the time they had paid about thirty thousand for each well-situated abode, a square meter of which is now worth millions. Enjoying quality health care and the other amenities of China's capital in addition to vacations abroad, they had come a long way since committing themselves to a life of labor alongside Xishuangbanna's poor and lower-middle peasants.

Like other Fifty-fivers—but unlike Xi Jinping—Li Saiyang was not able to coast through life in the filial footsteps of a Revolutionary icon. But Li's credentials were good enough to give him a running start. Born in Yan'an to parents who had married while serving Chairman Mao and the revolution, he had grown up in post-Liberation Beijing, where his father served as political secretary to a prominent official. He had become a CYL stalwart while still in middle school. By the time he was ready to graduate, he was a Party member—one of three in his student body. Following graduation, he was handpicked to undertake language study in France.

Chinese politics nullified these plans but opened new opportunities. When the Cultural Revolution erupted, Li posted his school's first Big Character Poster—but soon fell under attack as a stalwart of the Protect the Emperor faction of the Red Guards. His father and mother were struggled against and incarcerated. Desperately seeking an honorable and productive future, Li embarked upon the path to Yunnan spearheaded by classmate He Longkang. After detraining in Kunming, he and two comrades continued their journey on foot and by car, finally joining the Fifty-five in Xishuangbanna.

Though a new kid on the block, Li did not hesitate to confront leftist leaders during the "Beat the Drowning Dog" fracas. His reward for this display of courage was three years of hard labor in a lime kiln. During his decade in the countryside, Li nonetheless rose through Party ranks and was trusted with administrative tasks. As Party Secretary of a branch farm, he dared to defy leftist leaders by holding a high-profile memorial service for the late Zhou Enlai. Finally recognized as a rising star, he was sent to the Yunnan Provincial Party school. In 1979, he abandoned a budding provincial career to return to Beijing, fortunately accompanied by his Shanghai *zhiqing* wife. Li found work in the judicial administration of the Beijing City government. He soon gained an appointment to a judgeship while simultaneously enrolling in a part-time Beijing University legal studies program.

As one of a contingent of newly trained lawyers during the early period of reform, Li was assigned to the Beijing City Travel Office in charge of drafting legal documents and contracts for "joint venture" hotels and other enterprises launched in league with foreign companies, including Kentucky Fried Chicken. When an incompatible individual became his office head, however, Li found it difficult to continue. His case reveals a persistent motif of Chinese bureaucracy: Personal and factional relations between superiors and underlings trump bureaucratic imperatives that might otherwise pave the way to a successful career. Li's only option was to resign:

> I jumped into the sea. It must have been in 1990 or 1991. I went to work for the Kempinski Hotel. Later I joined the Institute for Research in Chinese Medicine, where I opened a clinic called the Chinese Medicine Institute Center for Medicine and Health Maintenance. Then I launched a legal office in this organization. In my career I had done everything. I had been a judge, lawyer, general manager, director of this, teacher of that, chairman of the board, secretary. As a lawyer, I was defense counsel on some big cases, including those of Beijing mayor Chen Xitong and of Li Min, head of the Beijing Office of Public Security.

Li Saiyang, like many of his generational cohort, had learned how to seize opportunities—playing along when the playing was good, getting out while the getting was good. Skills acquired during a decade of rural exile—adaptability, opportunism, awareness of an ever-changing environment full of possibilities but pockmarked with pitfalls—were precisely those needed for success in late twentieth-century Beijing. To these he added a social conscience that goaded him to serve his country and fellow citizens as well as himself. From his own experience, Li concluded that "the future development of Chinese history will not be brought about by a few individuals or leaders." Rejecting the official myth that all good things were gifts from above, he proclaimed that:

> Lots of historical events are not the work of heroes. Who brought them about? Hard-working people. I really don't credit any individual with creating Reform and Opening Up. Those are myths made up after the fact. Real Reform and Opening Up come from the hearts of the people and are the necessary product of people's actions.

"After these few decades," Li sees "two prominent achievements of reform: 1. We've learned the lessons of the Cultural Revolution. We've done away with lifelong tenure [for leaders]. Now there's talk again of revising the constitution. That would bring us nothing beneficial." (By the time of our interview, the Constitution had, in fact, been revised to allow President Xi lifelong tenure.) "The greatest fruits of reforms," declared Li, "have been private property and liberation of the economy. These things are protected by the nation." "There will inevitably be some twists and turns," he predicted, "but in the long run I'm optimistic. In the short run, however, I'm not optimistic. We might well move backward."

Appreciating the reluctance of Chinese to take stands on political issues, when interviewing the Fifty-fivers I assiduously avoided asking sensitive questions. Li, however, was far from bashful about sharing his views:

Some people say there have been three great migrations in recent Chinese history. The first was the flight to Hong Kong during the Cultural Revolution. At that time [Xi Jinping's father] Xi Zhongxun was Party Secretary in Guangdong. He dealt with this issue very appropriately. The second great migration occurred after the chaos [of the Cultural Revolution]—the migration of intellectuals. The third is happening now. Many people with capital, both financial and human capital, are now living abroad. And the person responsible for this third migration is Xi Zhongxun's son.

This is as close as any of my interviewees came to criticizing China's supreme leader by name.

Li judged China's social inequities to be the inevitable byproduct of an entrenched political elite:

There's too big a gulf between rich and poor. They don't understand each other. The rich live their own lives but forget about these other people. Their lives are so comfortable that they don't realize that not everyone lives the way they do. But if you want to address this problem, you need political reform. For example, eliminating lifelong tenure for our leaders. In so doing, you should uphold the advances that have been made in recent years, protect individual property rights, individual wealth, freedom of speech.

I emerged from my interview sensing that liberal democratic values might not be—as China's official media would have us believe—an unwelcome American import but may, rather, emerge from the experience of Xi Jinping's own generation.

Mr. Li was not alone in holding such views. Among those who sought me out were two women. A minority among the Fifty-fivers, the females were also younger, more likely going to Yunnan as sixteen-year-olds rather than as nineteen-year-olds. Outnumbered by the boys, the girls, with several notable exceptions, had been followers rather than leaders in the countryside, returning to Beijing as wives and mothers, shouldering household burdens that made it difficult to compete for education and jobs.

These two women had, nonetheless, retired from productive careers as technological specialists, what had been called, during the Mao years, "Experts"—in contrast to "Reds" who drew upon political skills. What they wanted most to share with me was not their professional experience but their views on social and political issues.

They had gone to the countryside as true believers, prepared to sacrifice everything for Maoist values. Lacking the revolutionary family background and political connections of some of their peers and suspected of harboring negative views of leftist bosses on the State Farm, these young women had found few opportunities to enter the Party or develop leadership skills.

Rather, they had become receptive to "bourgeois ideas" such as freedom, equality, and the rule of law.

They had returned to Beijing skeptical about Deng Xiaoping's claim that the benefits of allowing a few to get rich first would trickle down to China's masses. Recently retired, they now looked on with horror as "the leftist stuff" reemerged. In their eyes, Xi Jinping's ambition was "to become a second Mao." The problem with Xi and his coterie: "They are unwilling to give up their idea of a Red landscape."

These women looked askance as vast fortunes accumulated in the hands of a political-economic elite whose wealth was expatriated through children with foreign passports. As examples of the rottenness of the system, they cited Military Affairs Commission vice-chair Xu Caihou's expulsion from the Party for alleged corruption. They also decried the arbitrary use of state power, as exemplified by environmentalist Lei Yang, who had died in police custody following the accusation of soliciting sex—a routine practice among China's official/commercial elite.

How many former sent-down youth hold such critical views is impossible to ascertain. My dissident friends themselves found no consensus among the Fifty-five whom they characterized—in Sun Yat-sen's words—as "grains of loose sand." Others who agreed to interviews have, as noted, also expressed critical views, though seldom in such sweeping terms. The opinions of these people, while significant, are not representative sampling. I am fully aware that I was only able to interview those who responded to my call for volunteers during a luncheon attended by about half of the Fifty-fivers living in Beijing. Some, I was advised by a confidant, still saw me as an American with a suspicious agenda, someone to be avoided. Although I assiduously avoided questions of "hot" issues, it is striking that, in a country where sharing critical opinions with anybody, particularly a foreigner, can invite unpleasant consequences, some stepped forward to do just that.

Whatever the danger of speaking one's mind, some of the Fifty-five who had risked everything to serve their country during the Cultural Revolution remained, half a century later, unwilling to remain silent about injustice and inequity. Other interviewees, though less outspoken, convey a general belief that, despite access to various levels of decent housing, medical care, and opportunities to travel abroad, some things in China are not quite right. Even those reluctant to criticize politics, find ample reason to voice social critiques. Many accept what was, at the time, the officially approved portrayal of fellow countrymen as lacking in *wenming* (civility) and *suzhi* (personal moral character). Those who have traveled abroad are painfully aware that Chinese tourists are widely regarded as uncultivated boors who descend from tour buses with a deeper zeal for shopping than for cultural understanding. Xi

Figure 11.3. Author and Fifty-fivers in Beijing, 2018. (Chen Xinzeng collection)

Jinping's critique of official corruption draws support from many who do not necessarily endorse other aspects of his rule.

Revisiting Xishuangbanna, Fifty-fivers find evidence of social and economic injustice. When they arrived in the countryside half a century ago, the system opened a path for them to pursue their ideals, however unhappy the consequences. They were able to envision themselves playing a role in a national drama. Now, as retirees in Beijing, they lead comfortable lives but shrink back from seeing themselves in a larger national context. In rural Yunnan, however, realities are inescapable. Old friends no longer live on the edge of destitution but are far from enjoying anything approaching the minimum levels of material prosperity, economic security, and medical care taken for granted in the nation's capital.

In the Yunnan countryside *zhiqing* returnees discover the long-term consequences of the landscape they created. Shallow-rooted rubber trees that they planted after leveling triple-canopy tropical forests have fostered floods and soil erosion. Extreme climatic crises are frequent. Furthermore, wealth created by tourists, snowbirds, and urban émigrés has failed to trickle down to denizens of the mountainous countryside among whom they once lived and labored. With its high-rises and superhighways, today's Xishuangbanna is more modern but less attractive than the backward but romantic place where they spent their youthful years.

The China of Xi Jinping, in which survivors of the *zhiqing* generation are living out their retirements, is exponentially more prosperous and powerful than the China of Mao Zedong in which they grew up. But they now have fewer illusions about its future.

Figure 11.4. Fifty-fivers visit previous team leaders. (Wang Huimin Collection)

Figure 11.5. Revisiting rubber plantation with old State Farm worker. (You Heng collection)

Figure 11.6. Old comrades pay tribute to Ling Yu and Wang Kaiping. (Peng Ange collection)

Index

Note: Page numbers in *italics* reference Figures.

About the Author

Born in New York City in 1935, **John Israel** grew up in suburban Nassau County. After graduating from the University of Wisconsin in 1955, he studied Chinese history under John King Fairbank at Harvard University (MA 1957, PhD 1963). He is well known for his writings on students and higher education in twentieth-century China. Professor Israel conducted research in Taiwan and Hong Kong (1959–1962, 1973) and the People's Republic of China since 1980. Following the normalization of US-China diplomatic relations, he became the first post–1949 American resident professor in Kunming. Over the past four decades, he has lived and studied in China—particularly in Yunnan province—for extensive periods.